MW00576825

Tom Greenwood

SUSTAINABLE WEB DESIGN

MORE FROM A BOOK APART

Design for Cognitive Bias
David Dylan Thomas

Cross-Cultural Design
Senongo Akpem

Expressive Design Systems
Yesenia Perez-Cruz

Resilient Management
Lara Hogan

Everyday Information Architecture
Lisa Maria Marquis

Progressive Web Apps
Jason Grigsby

Flexible Typesetting
Tim Brown

Going Offline
Jeremy Keith

Conversational Design
Erika Hall

The New CSS Layout
Rachel Andrew

Visit abookapart.com for our full list of titles.

Copyright © 2021 Tom Greenwood
All rights reserved

Publisher: Jeffrey Zeldman
Designer: Jason Santa Maria
Executive director: Katel LeDû
Managing editor: Lisa Maria Marquis
Editor: Sally Kerrigan
Technical editor: Mat Marquis
Book producer: Ron Bilodeau

ISBN: 978-1-952616-03-7

A Book Apart
New York, New York
http://abookapart.com

10 9 8 7 6 5 4 3 2 1

TABLE OF CONTENTS

For future generations

FOREWORD

THE ONLY PROPER WAY to introduce the subject of this book is by first dismantling the idea that digital experiences are exempt from environmental costs. We create digital litter that has tangible consequences, manifesting as greenhouse gas emissions and factory waste. If the internet is a public space, then we ought to treat it as the most valuable of its kind—an internet that lacks organization and cleanliness should bring us discomfort the way a polluted watering hole or neglected public restroom would. Instead, we have been reckless in the way we move about that public space, jeopardizing its future and that of our physical world.

However, the growing popularity of both technology and climate action means the emergence of those who operate at their intersection. The very fact that this book was written is living proof that there is an audience for sustainable web design— perhaps a mix of technologists and designers and climate experts who have a metaphorical foot in both worlds. (As an internet-era professional who lives in this overlap myself, I often wonder which I am first: a member of the climate-concerned, or a digital designer.)

I suspect all of us who find ourselves here feel somewhat lost and even a little bit unsupervised in our forays into this work, though our egos may not allow us to admit it. Even the elementary principles of sustainable web design have yet to be popularized. This book, and its wonderful author Tom Greenwood, will hopefully be part of an exciting exposition to a generation concerned about the environmental impact of our online selves, and confident in how to grapple with it.

To the technological professional, to the advocates of the environment, and to the users of the web: may this be a companion to your own education on the complicated, beautiful, and tragic union between the internet and our natural environment.

—Rachel He

INTRODUCTION

> *There are professions more harmful than industrial design, but only very few of them. And possibly only one profession is phonier. Advertising design, in persuading people to buy things they don't need, with money they don't have, in order to impress others who don't care, is probably the phoniest field in existence today.*

VICTOR PAPANEK, WHO WROTE these words in his 1971 book *Design for the Real World*, was an early pioneer of what we now call sustainable design. Papanek rallied against the use of design as a tool to fuel consumerism, and asserted that designers have an opportunity, and a responsibility, to help create a better world.

Thirty years later, as an environmentally minded teenager studying product design at university, I was inspired by Papanek's work. I was passionate about pursuing a career in product design, but only if I could also be a part of the solution to the environmental crisis. I chose sustainable design as my thesis topic and spent my final year researching every tool, technique, book, regulation, and case study of sustainable product design. Keen to inspire other designers to pursue sustainable practices, I put all of this information on a website in the first online guide to sustainable product design (**FIG 0.1**). At a time when "product design" almost exclusively referred to the design and engineering of physical products and services, that website was one of my first steps into the digital world.

At the turn of the millennium, when anyone talked about digital products or services in the context of sustainability, it was mainly as a potential panacea to our trash-producing global consumer culture. When my wife Vineeta and I set up Wholegrain Digital in 2007, it was with the rationale that we wanted to move away from designing and engineering physical products that might end up in landfill. Digital design could never become physical trash, and so we felt safely on the side of good environmental practice with our digital studio.

Sustainability
Tools
Design Strategies
Advice

Welcome to ESPDesign.org, the online resource for professionals and students interested in Sustainable Product Design.

Originally 'Environmentally' Sustainable Product Design, ESP Design has recently been updated and changed to 'Entirely' Sustainable Product Design to represent the range of different factors involved in Sustainability.

The site contains background information about sustainable product design, practical information on *how* to design sustainable products and links to other useful resources.

FIG 0.1: When I created espdesign.org, product design still meant the design of "real things."

That attitude shifted in 2016, when I learned that the world's data centers use more electricity than the whole of the United Kingdom (http://bkaprt.com/swd/00-01/). Holy guacamole! There we were, conscientiously turning off the lights when we left a room to save energy, recycling our waste and offsetting our travel, oblivious to the fact that the seemingly harmless digital products we designed were "always on"—in our offices, in our homes, and in our pockets. I'm embarrassed to admit it took nearly a decade from starting the business before we thought to even ask how much energy websites actually *use*.

As we'll see in the chapters ahead, websites demand a great deal of electricity, and all that power has to come from somewhere. No longer can we dismiss these concerns as irrelevant. The time has come for digital professionals to take leadership in our industry and develop a culture where sustainability is fundamental to everything we do.

I must clarify that *sustainability* in this book refers to the sustainability of our natural environment and our urgent need to cut carbon emissions to keep those natural systems in balance. It's not that financial profit or social value don't matter. I've long subscribed to John Elkington's principle of the Triple Bottom Line, a concept he introduced in the early '90s to suggest that we should measure profit not just on a financial bottom line, but also measure the benefit of our business to society and to the natural environment.

I don't have to tell you that your business needs to be financially sustainable, and there are plenty of books written about human-centered design, accessible design, inclusive design, and other social aspects of design and tech. However, there's an eerie silence about digital technology and the environment. Nature is the source from which all else grows. Without it, there is no financial profit, no social value, and no digital industry.

Whatever your role in the digital sector, this book aims to provide a starting point to help you understand the issues of sustainability, as well as the tools, techniques, and processes that can help us to create sustainable digital products. We'll also look at how we can approach sustainability in the business side of digital, and how climate change may impact the internet itself. From this foundation, I hope we can all help to create a web fit for the future we all face.

1 WHAT IS SUSTAINABLE WEB DESIGN?

THE ENORMOUS AND COMPLEX system that makes it possible for you to read an email, visit a web page, search on Google, or watch the latest series of *The Crown*—acts which may involve your phone, computer, television, Wi-Fi routers, a local telecom network, global and national repeater stations, and data centers—uses electricity at every stage. If the internet were a country, it would be the sixth most polluting country in the world, with annual emissions similar to those of Germany (**FIG 1.1**) (http://bkaprt.com/swd/01-01/).

The number of people connected to the internet is growing rapidly, with Cisco predicting two-thirds of the world's population will be connected by 2023 (http://bkaprt.com/swd/01-03/). At a time when we need to be moving rapidly towards a zero-carbon economy, our hunger for data and web services is growing ever greater—as are our internet emissions. A 2018 paper published in the *Journal of Cleaner Production* estimated that communication technology will use 14 percent of global electricity by 2040, up from just under 4 percent in 2020 (http://bkaprt.com/swd/01-04/).

As web designers we have long been blessed by ever-increasing internet speeds and computing power. Ironically, as

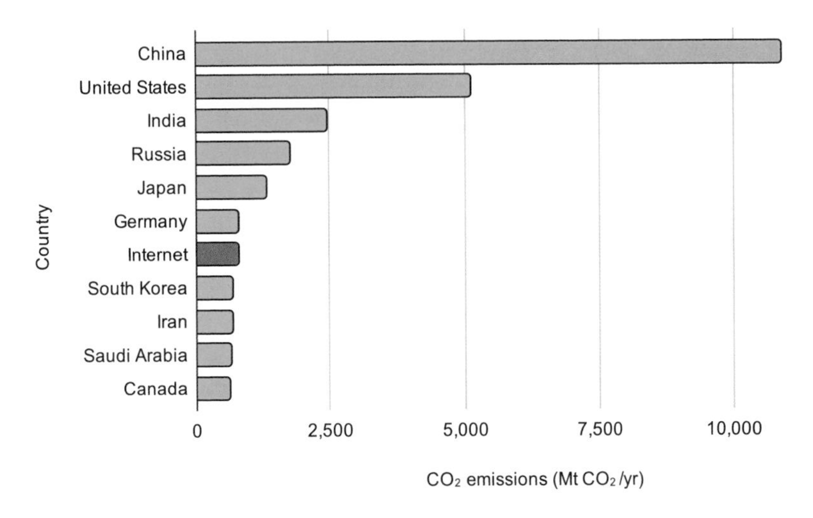

FIG 1.1: Data for 2018 shows that when viewed as a whole, the internet is equivalent to one of the world's most polluting countries (http://bkaprt.com/swd/01-02/).

computing and networks have become more efficient, we've tended to make increasingly power hungry and polluting websites. Like me just a few years ago, most of the web developers making these products simply didn't realize that digital services have an environmental impact. But past ignorance won't excuse continued inaction when the stakes are so high. If we wish to create web services that are good for people and the planet, we must take responsibility for the environmental impact of the work we do. This is what sustainable web design as a practice seeks to do.

Sustainable web design is an approach to designing web services that prioritizes the health of our home planet. At its core is a focus on reducing carbon emissions and energy consumption. What we need in every web project is a sustainability champion: at least one person who understands the issues, has some ideas for potential solutions, and can guide and encourage their fellow team members to consider sustainability at every stage of the project.

The principles and advice I've focused on here will equip you to become that champion in your own web design work.

As we'll see, in creating a web that's better for the planet, we'll create a web that's better for people, too.

FUNDAMENTAL PRINCIPLES FOR A SUSTAINABLE WEB

Sustainability initiatives tend to deliver incremental improvements that are bolted on to traditional ways of doing things. Radical and fundamental changes are what we need at this point to make sustainability part of the very fabric of design. That means we need to think about sustainability more deeply and be prepared to question the way that we have always done things.

In 2019, I coauthored the Sustainable Web Manifesto with a small group of fellow designers, developers, and digital professionals (**FIG 1.2**). The project aims to raise awareness of sustainability in our industry and sets out key principles we should consider in our work. It defines sustainable web projects as being clean, efficient, open, honest, regenerative, and resilient. Let's take a look at each of these to see what they mean in practice.

Clean

The first pledge in the Sustainable Web Manifesto states that all web projects should be clean, specifically in terms of energy use. The internet is almost entirely powered by electricity, and the more we use renewable energy sources such as solar, wind, wave, and hydroelectric to produce that power, the better.

We don't always have control over where the electricity for our projects comes from, but we often do have a choice over which hosting provider we use. The simplest way to make our projects environmentally clean is to select a host that has made a public commitment to using 100 percent renewable energy in their data centers.

We can't tell if a server is using renewable energy just by looking at it, but we can find out by asking the hosting company. The hosting providers already using renewable energy

FIG 1.2: I encourage you to read and sign it yourself at Sustainablewebmanifesto.com.

will be only too happy to tell you about it, and likely have information clearly presented on their website. For example, the homepage of the Positive Internet Company website states that their Positive Park data center "uses only green electricity sourced from 100 percent renewable sources" (http://bkaprt.com/swd/01-05/).

What about the energy used in the telecoms network and end user devices, and the energy used at the office where we work? We may have much less control over the other electricity used by our web projects, but it's possible to open the conversation about renewable energy by asking the right people. Maybe the company you work for is already using renewable energy but isn't talking about it enough, or maybe they would be open to it but haven't yet made it a priority. By being open about clean energy as a core value of sustainable web design, we can nudge progress in the right direction.

Efficient

Using clean energy is a great start, but with global data consumption growing at a rapid pace, the sheer volume of electricity used by the internet is jeopardizing any efforts to decarbonize our energy supplies. In every credible plan to tackle climate change, energy efficiency is one of the key strategies, and yet the internet's demand for energy shows no sign of slowing down.

It's easy to assume that our increasing consumption of data is purely due to people using the internet more, but that's only half the story—the other half shows that the websites and applications we build are becoming less efficient. As internet connection speeds get faster, and as computers and phones become increasingly powerful, we web professionals are unwittingly making our projects less efficient.

Working with powerful devices and speedy connections means we can get away with not sizing our images properly, with copying and pasting a whole library of code when we only need part of it, and with letting old, unnecessary lines clutter up our code. From 2017 to 2020, the median size of a web page increased by roughly 30 percent (http://bkaprt.com/swd/01-06/). Have websites really gotten 30 percent better? Sure, some of this increase in file sizes has contributed to richer online experiences, but much of it has done nothing to improve user experience, performance, or accessibility—quite the opposite!

When we make our web pages unnecessarily heavy and write queries that put extra load on servers and end users' devices, we are not just wasting electricity; we are wasting an opportunity to create faster and more inclusive online experiences. We must tackle this head-on and deliver great online experiences with minimal waste of resources.

Open

The creation of a truly sustainable web is going to need collaboration on a mass scale. As a web community we're particularly good at this; open source projects can help us to develop more robust solutions and spread them more rapidly, accelerating our ability to green the web as a community.

Greenpeace embraced this principle in their Planet 4 project, in which they redesigned the web platform used by their global teams using open principles, inviting open collaboration and publishing the full design and development process for others to learn from. The result was a web platform that in their own words is not just "a vehicle for putting content on the internet, but for driving people to action." The online handbook for the project acts "as the public, transparent and accessible placeholder for anyone who wants to help, learn or be inspired" (http://bkaprt.com/swd/01-07/).

In addition to fostering collaboration, openness allows us to learn from each other and makes important information more accessible. When we publish articles or present at conferences to share our attempts to make our web projects more sustainable, we help each other make progress. Openness allows us to stand on each other's shoulders and move forward as a community, building on progress rather than starting from nothing.

Openness can also help us to normalize the concept of sustainability and make it a part of the conversation in our industry, in much the same way user experience, performance, search engine optimization (SEO), and accessibility are common concepts we talk about daily. BBC Future offers a great example of this: at the bottom of each article on their website, they have started publishing the carbon emissions of the digital content (http://bkaprt.com/swd/01-08/). If such practices became commonplace, then web teams could include reducing carbon emissions as one of their criteria for how they judge the success of their own work.

The more open we are, the more we can be inspired by each other's successes, learn from each other's mistakes, and help each other do better. In doing so, we shorten the path to creating the sustainable, inclusive web we all want.

Honest

Honesty is the other side of the same coin as openness. We cannot be truly open unless we are also honest.

Whether we like to admit it or not, most money in web design is paying to promote a message, and it has real impact on human beliefs and behaviors. *Greenwashing* is the concept of making misleading claims to suggest you are helping the environment, when you're not. It is arguably one of the biggest threats to climate solutions, as organizations strive to make themselves look good and create a positive public image without actually doing the hard work required to become truly sustainable. Greenwashing lulls us all into a false sense of security by telling us what we want to hear. It might be reassuring in the short term, but it stands in the way of real progress.

One of the most prominent examples of greenwashing in recent history is the Volkswagen diesel scandal, known as Dieselgate (http://bkaprt.com/swd/01-09/). As awareness increased about the health risks of diesel emissions, governments started to enact tighter emission regulations on new diesel vehicles. In response, Volkswagen ran adverts to promote their "Clean Diesel" technology and create a positive public perception of their vehicles (**FIG 1.3**). The problem was that their clean diesel technology didn't really exist. Instead, they reprogrammed the engine management software for their diesel cars to cheat the government emissions tests. They had spent money telling the public a story about how they had solved the problem of diesel emissions, without actually solving the problem. They were eventually caught, but the scandal delayed progress to reduce vehicle emissions by several years.

Hannah Smith, a web developer with the climate action movement Extinction Rebellion, told me that the Honesty principle from the Sustainable Web Manifesto parallels the movement's first demand, "Tell the truth":

> *Facts and data are the known starting point for solving any problem effectively, be it a UX problem, a coding challenge, a customer complaint or, on a bigger level, tackling environmental problems. In the fight against climate change, if there was a more widespread awareness and embracement of the full truth of what's happening, I believe we'd all choose to live very differently.*

Honesty can also help us to develop more efficient and socially responsible online experiences. Dark patterns are subtle tricks used in websites and apps to make people buy or sign up for things they didn't mean to. It's a surprisingly common and unethical marketing technique, leading people to spend more time online, fueling needless consumerism, and harming the environment.

FIG 1.3: VW did a good job of making diesel look clean instead of actually making it clean.

Similarly, web services such as social media platforms are increasingly designed to encourage addictive behavior, while the harvesting of personal data can be used to target ads and influence minds in ways that are at best sneaky, and at worst downright sinister.

The common thread in all of these examples is that web services are frequently designed to manipulate beliefs and behaviors in intentionally dishonest ways. The consequences are far-reaching and can range from mental health issues in individuals, to the societal corruption of democracy, to the deterioration of the planet through increased internet use. When we're truthful with web users and do not seek to mislead or manipulate them, we not only serve the best interests of the people using our products, but also create a more environmentally sustainable web.

Regenerative

We've ignored the problems of climate change and species extinction for so long that simply doing no harm is no longer enough to be sustainable. At best, it will help us to avoid the worst effects of climate change, but it will not undo the damage we've already done and the impacts we've already set into motion.

This is why we need to shift our focus beyond the idea of harm mitigation to a new horizon in which our activities are truly regenerative, helping to heal and restore our natural ecosystems and society. This brings us to the concept of *redemptive technologies*, defined by Ursula Franklin in *The Real World of Technology* as technologies that help heal people and planet.

Can web design become a redemptive technology? How can web technology empower people to take meaningful action to restore our natural world?

Do Nation is a web app for encouraging healthy, environmentally friendly habits (**FIG 1.4**). Anyone can either make a pledge or run a campaign to raise pledges to do things like cycle to work, waste less food, or use reusable coffee cups. Their belief is that small actions add up to make a big difference—a difference far greater than the sum of their parts.

And they do! Do Nation has helped over twenty-one thousand people change almost seventy thousand habits, saving as much carbon as 6,150 flights from London to New York, many times more than the emissions of the web application itself. Founder Hermione Taylor reflected, "Ten to twenty years ago there was a flurry of local climate action campaigns running paper-based pledges—powerful as these were, they just weren't scalable or long-lasting. The automation of processes through digital technology has made it possible to create large scale positive impact."

We can also explore indirect forms of regeneration. For example, the search engine Ecosia uses profits from paid advertising to fund reforestation projects. The search engine itself does not actually help restore nature—it is after all just a search engine—but use of the search engine is directly linked to positive action to restore nature. Ecosia's homepage inspires with a running count of the total number of trees planted to date, and shows each user how many trees they have personally contributed by using Ecosia as their search engine. The numbers aren't just for show, either; Ecosia's FAQ documentation includes plentiful information about the science behind the reforestation initiatives they fund (**FIG 1.5**) (http://bkaprt.com/swd/01-10/).

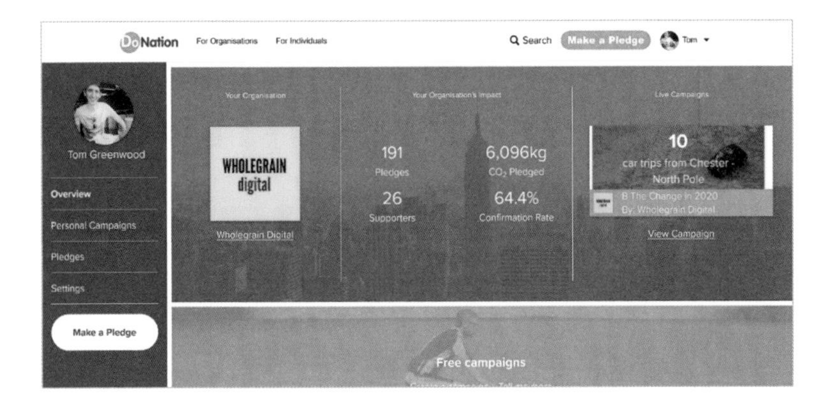

FIG 1.4: Do Nation has helped our team at Wholegrain Digital make small but meaningful lifestyle changes.

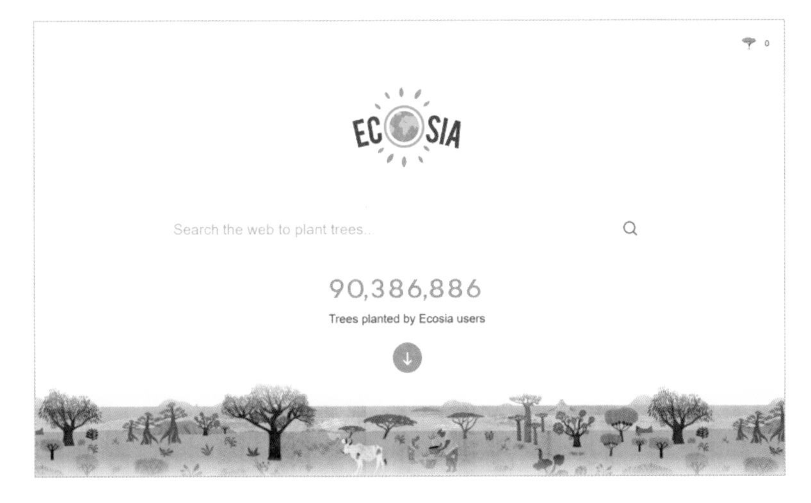

FIG 1.5: Ecosia has planted over 90 million trees and promotes best practice in ecosystem restoration projects.

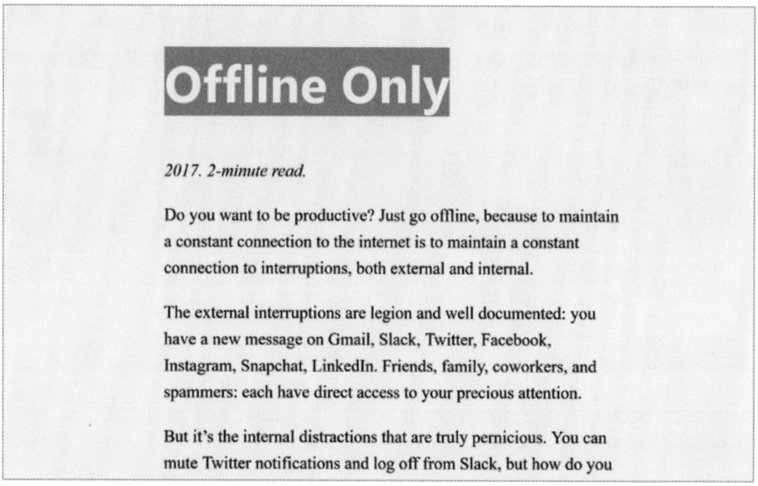

Offline Only

2017. 2-minute read.

Do you want to be productive? Just go offline, because to maintain a constant connection to the internet is to maintain a constant connection to interruptions, both external and internal.

The external interruptions are legion and well documented: you have a new message on Gmail, Slack, Twitter, Facebook, Instagram, Snapchat, LinkedIn. Friends, family, coworkers, and spammers: each have direct access to your precious attention.

But it's the internal distractions that are truly pernicious. You can mute Twitter notifications and log off from Slack, but how do you

FIG 1.6: You won't be able to see this page unless you switch your internet off.

Resilient

As climate change intensifies, the web will be a key tool in helping to ensure the resilience of society, helping us to rapidly share knowledge about the problems and the potential solutions.

In order for us to reap the benefits of the web in times of crisis, the web itself must be resilient enough to reliably serve information to the least privileged people in the worst affected areas. A resilient web is one in which key information and web services can be accessed on even the slowest connections, on any device, in almost any condition—from a moving vehicle to a natural disaster. Resilient web design avoids single points of failure and embraces graceful degradation of technology so that if one part of the system fails, key information can still be delivered to the user and remain fit for purpose, even if more advanced functionality is lost.

Software engineer Chris Bolin created a website that can only be accessed when the user is disconnected from the internet (**FIG 1.6**) (http://bkaprt.com/swd/01-11/). He was trying to emphasize how we need to take more time offline, away from the distractions of social media and messaging apps. In the process, he also demonstrated rather beautifully how we can create experiences in the web browser that work even if an internet connection is completely lost. It shows how websites, although *from* the web, do not always need to be connected to it. Embracing this concept is just one way we can create more resilient web services.

OUR ROLES IN SUSTAINABLE WEB DESIGN

Although the stakes are high when it comes to the health of our home planet, we must not undermine our efforts with an all-or-nothing approach in which nothing less than perfection will do. One thing I can guarantee is that nothing any of us will do will be perfect. The challenge is for all of us to see how close we can get. We all have a role to play in creating a sustainable web, whatever our job may be in the world of digital.

In traditional industries, the typical approach to making a business environmentally sustainable has been to bring in consultants to measure inputs and outputs, write reports, and advise on actions that could help achieve improvements. While this is great in many ways, we can see from lack of real progress in tackling climate change that it's not entirely effective. More radical change is needed, and the organizations that have made big steps forward in sustainability are those which don't just treat sustainability as icing on the cake, but as fundamental to the entire cake-making process.

Consider Ecover, the Belgian company that pioneered eco-friendly cleaning products. The business was founded in 1979 by a group of scientists who were shocked by the damage modern cleaning chemicals were doing to aquatic life (http://bkaprt.com/swd/01-12/). Sustainability has permeated every aspect of the business for over forty years. Their green-roofed factory in Malle is constructed from 90 percent recycled and renewable materials, and is close to becoming one of the first genuinely zero-waste factories in the world (http://bkaprt.com/swd/01-13/). In 2001, Ecover gave away their biodegradable formula in an ad campaign, challenging the competition to copy their technology

FIG 1.7: Authentic grounding in environmental values makes for bold messaging and brand identity for Ecover. Photo courtesy of Ecover.

"for nature's sake" (**FIG 1.7**). Ecover concept director Peter Malaise said at the time, "If even one of the major brands adopted our formula it would make a huge impact on the environment" (http://bkaprt.com/swd/01-14/).

They've led the cleaning industry in sustainability, and at the same time, have grown to become a household name all over Europe, competing head-on with global giants like Unilever, who are now trying to compete on green credentials (http://bkaprt.com/swd/01-15/).

Patagonia is another example of a company putting sustainability at the core of what it does, with a mission statement that plainly says, "We are in business to save our home planet." Founder Yvon Chouinard told Fast Company that in order to ensure this mission is embedded throughout the business, he has told their HR department, "Whenever we have a job opening, all things being equal, hire the person who's committed to saving the planet, no matter what the job is" (http://bkaprt.com/swd/01-16/).

This commitment to sustainability has led to some pretty bold actions, including:

- The use and development of eco-friendly textiles such as recycled polyester fleece and natural rubber wetsuits (http://bkaprt.com/swd/01-17/).
- Using profits to help fund environmental activism, through grants to grassroots environmental activists (http://bkaprt.com/swd/01-18/), and cofounding the nonprofit 1% For The Planet to certify organizations who donate 1 percent of their own revenue to environmental charities (http://bkaprt.com/swd/01-19/).
- Creating their own film department and producing environmental documentary films such as Damnation, a film created to raise awareness to help protect Europe's last natural rivers (http://bkaprt.com/swd/01-20/).
- Launching a program for refurbishing worn Patagonia clothes, originally called Common Threads and now called Worn Wear, which was launched with an advert in the *New York Times* on Black Friday 2011 telling customers to protect the environment by *not* buying new clothes from them (http://bkaprt.com/swd/01-21/, http://bkaprt.com/swd/01-22/). The Worn Wear website explains the benefits of buying used and how to trade in your old clothes—and perhaps most importantly, it makes used clothes look as appealing as new (**FIG 1.8**).

Companies like Ecover and Patagonia show us what can be achieved when we treat sustainability as a priority and not an afterthought. In web design and development, we can learn from this and likewise embed sustainability into everything we do. Let's use sustainability as a catalyst for creating fundamentally better web products and services—not just for the environment, but for the people who use the web and the organizations providing services through it.

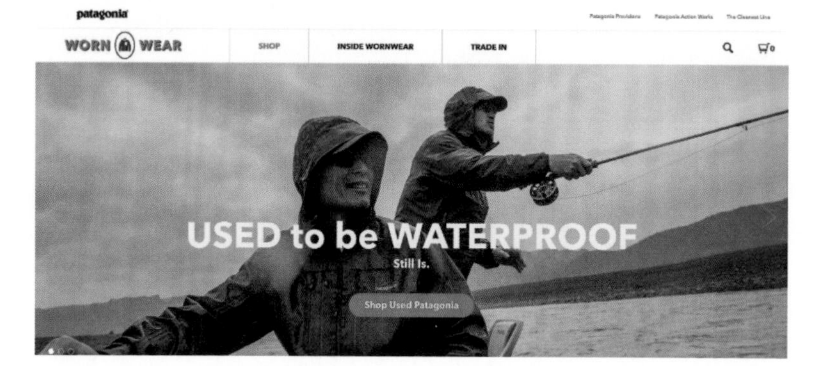

FIG 1.8: Patagonia Worn Wear sells refurbished clothes through a website that makes you feel that the clothes really are as good as new.

IS THIS OUR PROBLEM?

It could be argued that sustainability is not the job of web professionals to solve. We just build the products and services people want to use. Surely it's the consumer's responsibility to use the internet wisely, to buy low energy devices and use their data frugally.

This concept has been adopted by pretty much every industry when facing up to its own environmental impact. It started in the 1950s when the American Can Company, Owens-Illinois Glass Company, Coca-Cola, and the Dixie Cup Company got together to design a solution to the growing pressure to regulate disposable packaging. They knew the issue of litter would not go away and was increasingly unpopular with the public, but disposable packaging was incredibly profitable (http://bkaprt.com/swd/01-23/).

They needed a way to avoid regulation that might limit use of disposables, and their solution was cunning. They founded a nonprofit called Keep America Beautiful and poured significant amounts of money into environmental awareness campaigns. This helped make them look good, but the real genius was in the message behind the campaigns—that litter on the streets had nothing to do with the producers, but was the fault of the person who dropped it—*the litter bug*. Keep America Beautiful managed to shift the entire debate around America's garbage and litter problems away from the industry and onto consumers, and this strategy has been copied time and time again since.

We *could* do that as a digital industry, and it would probably work in diverting some unwanted pressure away from our sector, but like the other industries that have taken this approach, it would also divert attention away from actually solving the issues that matter. It's "good" marketing, but it's not good behavior.

Another argument is that it's the responsibility of the government to tackle the environmental issues relating to the internet. I've heard it claimed that individual professionals and organizations cannot make any impact on their own, and that regulation is needed to limit the industry's impact. We should remember the words of anthropologist Margaret Mead: "Never doubt that a small group of thoughtful, committed citizens can change the world; indeed, it's the only thing that ever has." So if government intervention is needed, it should not be *instead* of individual efforts, but *in addition* to it.

So, yes, it is our problem, and while no single web project is likely to "solve" everything at once, we each play a part.

In the face of the epic challenge of responding to the climate emergency, success will depend on every single one of us taking individual action and collaborating with those around us to have a real impact that's bigger than the sum of our individual parts. We all have a role to play, and together we can create a web that serves the needs of society for generations to come.

2 MEASURING OUR IMPACT

IN THE 1950S, MANY IN THE elite running community had begun to believe it wasn't possible to run a mile in less than four minutes. Runners had been attempting it since the late 19th century and were beginning to draw the conclusion that the human body simply wasn't built for the task.

But on May 6, 1956, Roger Bannister took everyone by surprise. It was a cold, wet day in Oxford, England—conditions no one expected to lend themselves to record-setting—and yet Bannister did just that, running a mile in 3:59.4 and becoming the first person in the record books to run a mile in under four minutes.

This shift in the benchmark had profound effects; the world now knew that the four-minute mile was possible. Bannister's record lasted only forty-six days, when it was snatched away by Australian runner John Landy. Then a year later, three runners all beat the four-minute barrier together in the same race. Since then, over 1,400 runners have officially run a mile in under four minutes; the current record is 3:43.13, held by Moroccan athlete Hicham El Guerrouj (http://bkaprt.com/swd/02-01/).

We achieve far more when we believe that something is possible, and we will believe it's possible only when we see someone else has already done it—and as with human running speed, so it is with what we believe are the hard limits for how a website needs to perform.

ESTABLISHING STANDARDS FOR A SUSTAINABLE WEB

In most major industries, the key metrics of environmental performance are fairly well established, such as miles per gallon for cars or energy per square meter for homes. The tools and methods for calculating those metrics are standardized as well, which keeps everyone on the same page when doing environmental assessments. In the world of websites and apps, however, we aren't held to any particular environmental standards, and only recently have gained the tools and methods we need to even make an environmental assessment.

The primary goal in sustainable web design is to reduce *carbon emissions*. However, it's almost impossible to actually measure the amount of CO_2 produced by a web product. We can't measure the fumes coming out of the exhaust pipes on our laptops. The emissions of our websites are far away, out of sight and out of mind, coming out of power stations burning coal and gas. We have no way to trace the electrons from a website or app back to the power station where the electricity is being generated and actually know the exact amount of greenhouse gas produced. So what do we do?

If we can't measure the actual carbon emissions, then we need to find what we *can* measure. The primary factors that could be used as indicators of carbon emissions are:

1. Data transfer
2. Carbon intensity of electricity

Let's take a look at how we can use these metrics to quantify the energy consumption, and in turn the carbon footprint, of the websites and web apps we create.

Data transfer

Most researchers use kilowatt-hours per gigabyte (kWh/GB) as a metric of energy efficiency when measuring the amount of data transferred over the internet when a website or application is used. This provides a great reference point for energy consumption and carbon emissions. As a rule of thumb, the more data transferred, the more energy used in the data center, telecoms networks, and end user devices.

For web pages, data transfer for a single visit can be most easily estimated by measuring the *page weight,* meaning the transfer size of the page in kilobytes the first time someone visits the page. It's fairly easy to measure using the developer tools in any modern web browser. Often your web hosting account will include statistics for the total data transfer of any web application (**FIG 2.1**).

The nice thing about page weight as a metric is that it allows us to compare the efficiency of web pages on a level playing field without confusing the issue with constantly changing traffic volumes.

Reducing page weight requires a large scope. By early 2020, the median page weight was 1.97 MB for setups the HTTP Archive classifies as "desktop" and 1.77 MB for "mobile," with desktop increasing 36 percent since January 2016 and mobile page weights nearly doubling in the same period (http://bkaprt.com/swd/02-02/) (**FIG 2.2**). Roughly half of this data transfer is image files, making images the single biggest source of carbon emissions on the average website.

History clearly shows us that our web pages *can* be smaller, if only we set our minds to it. While most technologies become ever more energy efficient, including the underlying technology of the web such as data centers and transmission networks, websites themselves are a technology that becomes less efficient as time goes on.

You might be familiar with the concept of performance budgeting as a way of focusing a project team on creating faster user experiences. For example, we might specify that the website must load in a maximum of one second on a broadband connection and three seconds on a 3G connection. Much like

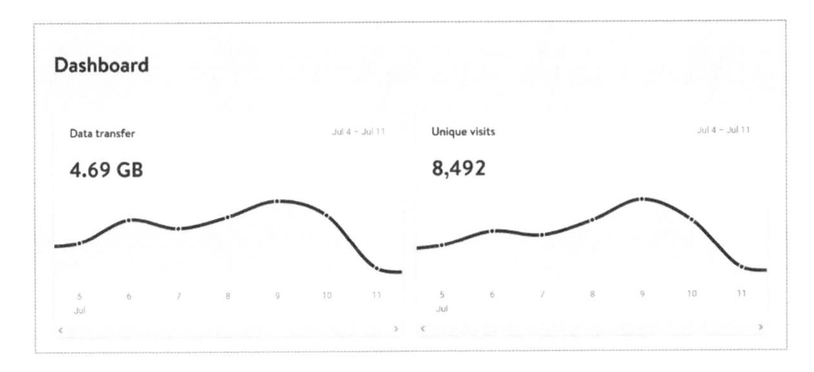

FIG 2.1: The Kinsta hosting dashboard displays data transfer alongside traffic volumes. If you divide data transfer by visits, you get the average data per visit, which can be used as a metric of efficiency.

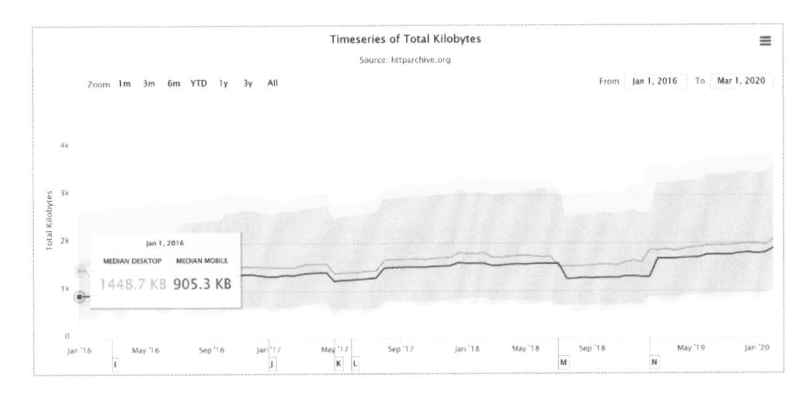

FIG 2.2: The historical page weight data from HTTP Archive can teach us a lot about what is possible in the future.

speed limits while driving, performance budgets are upper limits rather than vague suggestions, so the goal should always be to come in under budget.

Designing for fast performance does often lead to reduced data transfer and emissions, but it isn't always the case. Web performance is often more about the subjective perception of load times than it is about the true efficiency of the underlying system, whereas page weight and transfer size are more objective measures and more reliable benchmarks for sustainable web design.

We can set a page weight budget in reference to a benchmark of industry averages, using data from sources like HTTP Archive. We can also benchmark page weight against competitors or the old version of the website we're replacing. For example, we might set a maximum page weight budget as equal to our most efficient competitor, or we could set the benchmark lower to guarantee we are best in class.

If we want to take it to the next level, then we could also start looking at the transfer size of our web pages for repeat visitors. Although page weight for the first time someone visits is the easiest thing to measure, and easy to compare on a like-for-like basis, we can learn even more if we start looking at transfer size in other scenarios too. For example, visitors who load the same page multiple times will likely have a high percentage of the files cached in their browser, meaning they don't need to transfer all of the files on subsequent visits. Likewise, a visitor who navigates to new pages on the same website will likely not need to load the full page each time, as some global assets from areas like the header and footer may already be cached in their browser. Measuring transfer size at this next level of detail can help us learn even more about how we can optimize efficiency for users who regularly visit our pages, and enable us to set page weight budgets for additional scenarios beyond the first visit.

Page weight budgets are easy to track throughout a design and development process. Although they don't actually tell us carbon emission and energy consumption analytics directly, they give us a clear indication of efficiency relative to other websites. And as transfer size is an effective analog for energy consumption, we can actually use it to estimate energy consumption too.

In summary, reduced data transfer translates to energy efficiency, a key factor to reducing carbon emissions of web products. The more efficient our products, the less electricity they use, and the less fossil fuels need to be burned to produce the electricity to power them. But as we'll see next, since all web products demand *some* power, it's important to consider the source of that electricity, too.

Carbon intensity of electricity

Regardless of energy efficiency, the level of pollution caused by digital products depends on the *carbon intensity* of the energy being used to power them. Carbon intensity is a term used to define the grams of CO_2 produced for every kilowatt-hour of electricity (gCO_2/kWh). This varies widely, with renewable energy sources and nuclear having an extremely low carbon intensity of less than 10 gCO_2/kWh (even when factoring in their construction); whereas fossil fuels have very high carbon intensity of approximately 200–400 gCO_2/kWh (http://bkaprt.com/swd/02-03/, http://bkaprt.com/swd/02-04/).

Most electricity comes from national or state grids, where energy from a variety of different sources is mixed together with varying levels of carbon intensity. The distributed nature of the internet means that a single user of a website or app might be using energy from multiple different grids simultaneously; a website user in Paris uses electricity from the French national grid to power their home internet and devices, but the website's data center could be in Dallas, USA, pulling electricity from the Texas grid, while the telecoms networks use energy from everywhere between Dallas and Paris.

We don't have control over the full energy supply of web services, but we do have some control over where we host our projects. With a data center using a significant proportion of the energy of any website, locating the data center in an area with low carbon energy will tangibly reduce its carbon emissions. Danish startup Tomorrow reports and maps this user-contributed data, and a glance at their map shows how, for example, choosing a data center in France will have significantly lower carbon emissions than a data center in the Netherlands (**FIG 2.3**) (http://bkaprt.com/swd/02-05/).

That said, we don't want to locate our servers too far away from our users; it takes energy to transmit data through the telecom's networks, and the further the data travels, the more energy is consumed. Just like food miles, we can think of the distance from the data center to the website's core user base as "megabyte miles"—and we want it to be as small as possible.

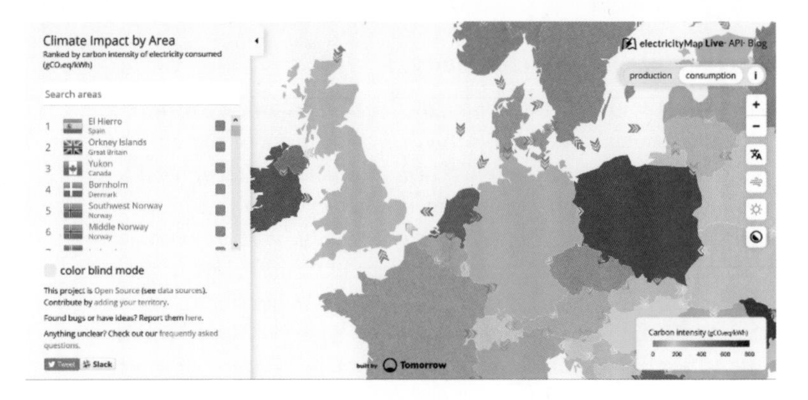

FIG 2.3: Tomorrow's electricityMap shows live data for the carbon intensity of electricity by country.

Using the distance itself as a benchmark, we can use website analytics to identify the country, state, or even city where our core user group is located and measure the distance from that location to the data center used by our hosting company. This will be a somewhat fuzzy metric as we don't know the precise center of mass of our users or the exact location of a data center, but we can at least get a rough idea.

For example, if a website is hosted in London but the primary user base is on the West Coast of the USA, then we could look up the distance from London to San Francisco, which is 5,300 miles. That's a long way! We can see that hosting it somewhere in North America, ideally on the West Coast, would significantly reduce the distance and thus the energy used to transmit the data. In addition, locating our servers closer to our visitors helps reduce latency and delivers better user experience, so it's a win-win.

Converting it back to carbon emissions

If we combine carbon intensity with a calculation for energy consumption, we can calculate the carbon emissions of our websites and apps. A tool my team created does this by measuring the data transfer over the wire when loading a web page, cal-

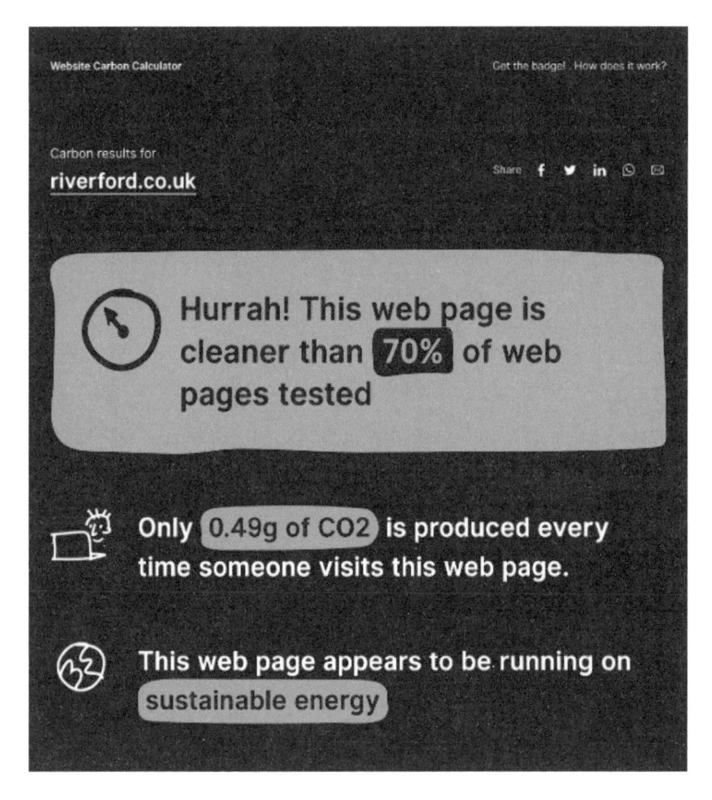

FIG 2.4: The Website Carbon Calculator shows how the Riverford Organic website embodies their commitment to sustainability, being both low carbon and hosted in a data center using renewable energy (http://bkaprt.com/swd/02-07/).

culating the amount of electricity associated, and then converting that into a figure for CO_2 (**FIG 2.4**). It also factors in whether or not the web hosting is powered by renewable energy.

If you want to take it to the next level and tailor the data more accurately to the unique aspects of your project, the Energy and Emissions Worksheet accompanying this book shows you how (http://bkaprt.com/swd/02-06/).

With the ability to calculate carbon emissions for our projects, we could actually take a page weight budget one step further and set carbon budgets as well. CO_2 is not a metric commonly used in web projects; we're more familiar with kilobytes and megabytes, and can fairly easily look at design options and files to assess how big they are. Translating that into carbon adds a layer of abstraction that isn't as intuitive—but carbon budgets do focus our minds on the primary thing we're trying to reduce, and support the core objective of sustainable web design: reducing carbon emissions.

Browser Energy

Data transfer might be the simplest and most complete analog for energy consumption in our digital projects, but by giving us one number to represent the energy used in the data center, the telecoms networks, and the end user's devices, it can't offer us insights into the efficiency in any specific part of the system.

One part of the system we can look at in more detail is the energy used by end users' devices. As front-end web technologies become more advanced, the computational load is increasingly moving from the data center to users' devices, whether they be phones, tablets, laptops, desktops, or even smart TVs. Modern web browsers allow us to implement more complex styling and animation on the fly using CSS and JavaScript. Furthermore, JavaScript libraries such as Angular and React allow us to create applications where the "thinking" work is done partly or entirely in the browser.

All of these advances are exciting and open up new possibilities for what the web can do to serve society and create positive experiences. However, more computation in the user's web browser means more energy used by their devices. This has implications not just environmentally, but also for user experience and inclusivity. Applications that put a heavy processing load on the user's device can inadvertently exclude users with older, slower devices and cause batteries on phones and laptops to drain faster. Furthermore, if we build web applications that require the user to have up-to-date, powerful devices, people throw away old devices much more frequently. This isn't just bad for the environment, but it puts a disproportionate financial burden on the poorest in society.

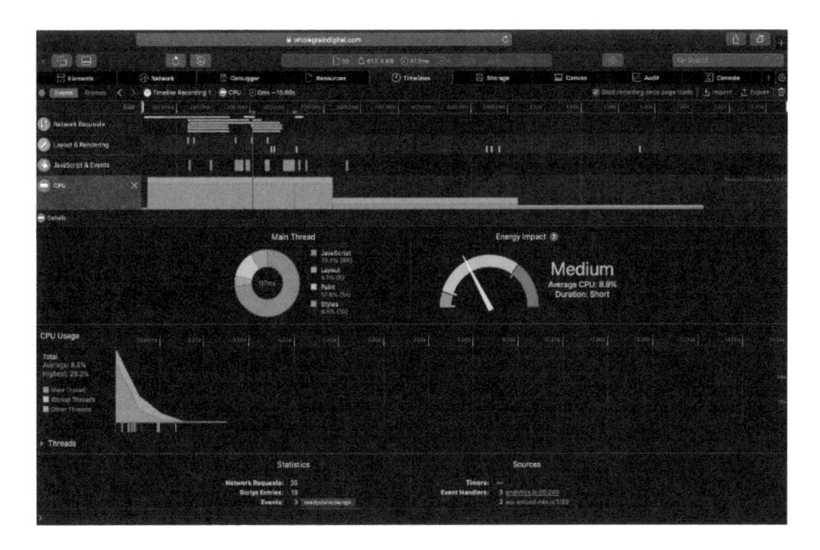

FIG 2.5: The Energy Impact meter in Safari (on the right) shows how a website consumes CPU energy.

In part because the tools are limited, and partly because there are so many different models of devices, it's difficult to measure website energy consumption on end users' devices. One tool we do currently have is the Energy Impact monitor inside the developer console of the Safari browser (**FIG 2.5**).

You know when you load a website and your computer's cooling fans start spinning so frantically you think it might actually take off? That's essentially what this tool is measuring.

It shows us the percentage of CPU used and the duration of CPU usage when loading the web page, and uses these figures to generate an energy impact rating. It doesn't give us precise data for the amount of electricity used in kilowatts, but the information it does provide can be used to benchmark how efficiently your websites use energy and set targets for improvement.

HOW TO USE SUSTAINABILITY BENCHMARKS

So how do you go about using benchmarks to improve the sustainability of your web projects? First, you have to decide which metrics you are going to focus on, depending on what seems most relevant to your project and what data you have access to.

For each metric, the *ideal* figure to minimize emissions would be zero. The ideal amount of data transfer to minimize emissions is 0 KB, the ideal amount of data storage is 0 MB, and the ideal distance from data center to web visitor is zero miles. You get the idea—if all the figures are zero, then the carbon emissions will also be zero.

I bet you're thinking this doesn't seem realistic, and you'd be right! It might be true that the most ecofriendly website is the one that doesn't exist, but as web designers and developers, that's not particularly helpful advice. We therefore need to use these metrics to challenge ourselves to see how low we can go without compromising the core requirements of the products we're creating.

I recommend the following steps for setting a sustainability budget for each of your chosen metrics:

- **Benchmark.** Measure the relevant metrics of equivalent web pages. This would ideally be the current version of a page you're redesigning, if there is one, and the equivalent pages on your competitors' websites. This shows you the variation within your industry for presenting equivalent information, and allows you to benchmark the current best practice in your industry.
- **Estimate what's possible.** The benchmark you've established tells you what has currently been achieved, but it doesn't tell you what is theoretically possible. Now, we must estimate what is theoretically possible in a best-case scenario. For example, you might estimate the best possible page weight by using your CMS to create a basic web page using written content but no videos, images, custom webfonts, or tracking scripts.
- **Set your budget.** Now that we know what is normal, what is the current best practice in our sector, and the theoretical

best-case scenario, we have the perspective from which we can set a budget for our chosen metrics. We should set a budget that's at least as good as the current best in our industry, and ideally stretch ourselves a little to improve on this. If the best in our industry is close to the theoretical best case, then we might not have much room for improvement, but if there is a huge gap between these two figures, then we have the opportunity to set new standards in our sector. The important thing to note is that the budget for each metric should be one you are confident is achievable. That way, we know we're setting ourselves up for success.
- **Set a stretch goal.** While the budget for each metric sets a hard limit that you know is achievable and are committed not to exceed, I encourage you to be more ambitious. Set yourself a stretch goal for each metric you know will be difficult, but theoretically possible. This not only helps push you to deliver higher levels of efficiency, it also gives you an interesting challenge.

What's the smallest possible footprint a website can have and still be functional? Benchmarking web projects and striving for new records inevitably leads us to produce work that performs better. With tools and methods to make an assessment, we can work towards a future where sustainability is a standard goal of any web design project.

THE EMBODIED CARBON OF DIGITAL PROJECTS

We've seen how digital products and services produce carbon emissions through their use of electricity, but that's not the only carbon impact we have as web professionals in doing the work we do. We also produce emissions through our day-to-day operations.

In the world of physical products, there's a term for the carbon emitted in producing the product and getting it to the customer: *embodied carbon*. It includes the energy used to produce the materials, manufacture the product, package it, and transport it. For example, a basic iPhone 11 (which weighs 194 grams) has a carbon footprint of 72 kg CO_2 over its entire life. However, only 17 percent of the carbon emissions occur when the phone is being used by the person who bought it. The remaining 83 percent of the total emissions are the embodied carbon from manufacture, transport, and end of life disposal (http://bkaprt.com/swd/02-08/, PDF). This highlights the importance of looking at the embodied carbon, and not just the emissions of a product in use.

In the world of digital products and services, we don't need to forge steel, mold plastic or mill paper, nor do we need to put our websites into containers and ship them from a factory to our customers. But that doesn't mean our web products don't have any embodied carbon. The embodied carbon of a website comes from everything we do in our day-to-day work—our computers, our lighting, our heating, our air conditioning, our commute to the office, our travel to see our clients and yes, those endless cups of tea and coffee.

The question is, what has a bigger impact—the emissions from our digital products, or the embodied carbon resulting from our physical operations?

Emission scenarios

Let's look at some example scenarios to compare the impact of different types of digital projects relative to the emissions of physical activities (**FIG 2.6**). I've charted the annual carbon emissions for low-, medium-, and high-carbon-efficiency websites according to low-, medium-, and high-traffic scenarios (ten thousand, one hundred thousand, and one million visitors per month, respectively). Compare these numbers to the emissions of round-trip flights from London to Paris and from London to San Francisco (using data from carbonfootprint.com), as well as the annual non-digital emissions from our operations at Wholegrain Digital.

So what causes the most emissions? It's clear that a high-traffic, low-carbon-efficiency website can have a very large impact—in this case, exceeding our business operations emissions at Wholegrain Digital. We can also see that business operations and a long-distance flight have a significant impact.

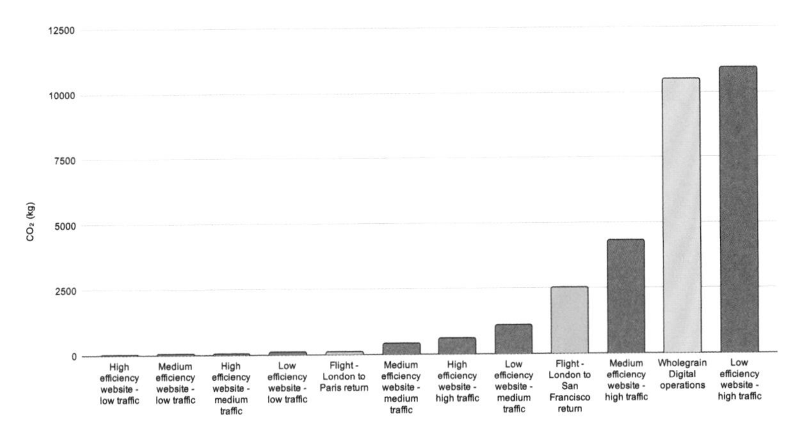

FIG 2.6: For these calculations, the high- and low-carbon-efficiency website data come from real websites (gtrailway.com and thesun.co.uk, respectively), and the medium-carbon-efficiency example comes from average data from HTTParchive.org.

However, it's also apparent that high-carbon-efficiency websites, even with high traffic, have a relatively low impact.

For some of us, digital emissions may have a bigger impact than this chart illustrates if we're involved in creating and maintaining several websites per year. At the same time, some may have a higher carbon footprint from physical emissions if they fly a lot for business. Both the emissions of our physical activities *and* the emissions of our digital projects are truly significant. We cannot pick one and ignore the other as if it doesn't matter.

Looking at these scenarios, it's important to note that although traffic has a big impact on digital emissions, we often *want* to create websites that attract high traffic volumes. Therefore, the pursuit of carbon efficiency in our websites is the single most important factor to help us keep digital emissions low. And this doesn't just apply to whole websites. The same is true if you create code or design templates used by lots of other websites.

For example, developer Danny van Kooten analyzed the carbon emissions of several WordPress plugins he created and found that removing a 20 KB JavaScript dependency from the

Mailchimp for WordPress plugin—installed on two million websites—would reduce emissions by 708 tons per year (**FIG 2.7**) (http://bkaprt.com/swd/02-09/). He concluded that while it's good to reduce his carbon footprint in all aspects of his life, optimizing his digital products was by far the best way he could help tackle climate change.

We all have different working arrangements and work on different types of projects, so it's important to look at the broad picture of our carbon emissions and identify where we can make a difference. Tools like Carbon Footprint make it easier to estimate the emissions from our travel and energy use, which we can then review in the context of our digital emissions in order to make informed choices on how we can make a positive impact (http://bkaprt.com/swd/02-10/).

DEFINING GOOD

If we are to do good work, then we must know what "good" means in the context of sustainable web design. In a broad sense, sustainable design *is* good design, but we must have a way of *measuring* sustainability in order to make tangible progress. When we use metrics and tools to quantify the environmental impact of our web projects and day-to-day operations, we can understand our impact and create a vision for what "good" looks like. As we saw with Roger Bannister's four-minute mile, benchmarking performance inspires us to take things to the next level and achieve what was previously considered impossible. If we include environmental benchmarking in our web projects, we can set goals to push ourselves to continuously do better.

3 DESIGNING LOW-CARBON WEBSITES

A COMMON PROBLEM IN web projects, especially when there are a lot of stakeholders, is that we end up including far more than is necessary because we're afraid of leaving something out.

We're afraid of missing an opportunity. We're afraid of upsetting or frustrating the user. Or, in many cases, we're afraid of having to say no to colleagues who suggested the idea in the first place. Implementing a minimalist approach is hard. It involves a degree of ruthlessness to cut things out and say no to ideas that can't be justified. It requires us to not give every idea and every piece of content the benefit of the doubt, but instead to say, "If in doubt, we're going to leave it out."

Our internet connections continually become faster and cheaper, making the problem worse as we web designers become more complacent when it comes to considering efficiency. It's like packing for holiday; when travelling by train, I am always vigilant about every item I take, because I know I will have to carry it—but when travelling by car? I just throw it all in. Not because I need it, but because it's easy to be complacent. *Yoga mat? Extra shoes? Smoothie maker? Sure, chuck it all in!*

We've been designing websites with the mindset of someone packing for a road trip in the family SUV, not for a backpacking

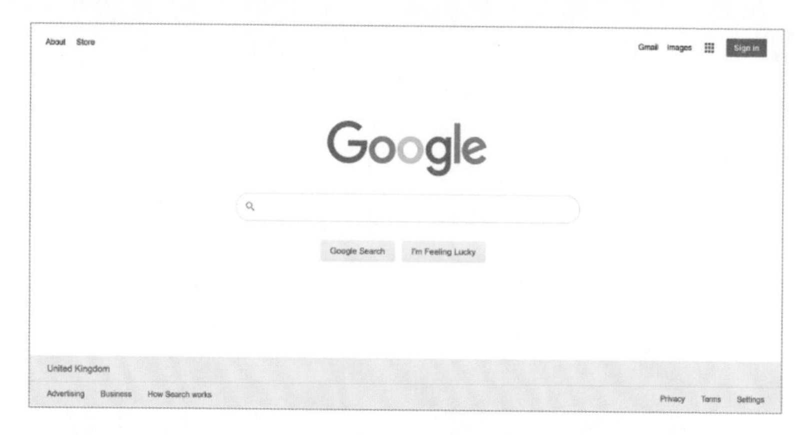

FIG 3.1: The Google homepage is a great example of web design coming as close to "nothing" as possible.

trip by train. We must shift our perspective to focus on efficiency if we are to design a sustainable web.

When we view decisions through the lens of sustainability from the very beginning of the web design process, it elevates our thinking and challenges our ideas on a deeper level. We must justify the existence of every element, no longer asking, "Would this be nice to add?" but instead, "Can we live without it?" It requires assessment of every detail of a design solution from images to text to pages and content. It is minimalism in its purest form.

Minimalist web design doesn't mean our designs have to be bare and stark. It simply means we should justify the existence of every detail in the work we produce. We want to get as close to "nothing" as possible while still delivering a positive, intuitive, and useful experience to the user. The Google homepage is a great example of this, focusing on delivering the core functionality in the simplest way possible (**FIG 3.1**).

It might be difficult, but when we have the guts to pursue a less-is-more approach, the rewards extend far beyond the reduced environmental footprint. We create online experiences that load faster, are easier to access on patchy connections, are faster to develop, and offer more streamlined and intuitive user journeys. We need to stop using FOMO as the guiding principle of web design and embrace the idea that in a world of information overload, our users will thank us for cutting out the clutter.

With this in mind, let's look at some of the key elements of digital design to understand how a sustainable design approach yields great results for people and planet.

SIMPLIFY THE USER EXPERIENCE

Information architects and user experience designers have considerable influence over the environmental impact of a website. Even if sustainability is ignored completely in all subsequent stages of the project, leading to bloated designs, inefficient code, and the most polluting hosting, good information architecture (IA) and user experience (UX) can limit the impact of those later decisions. In fact, the less attention paid to sustainability in later stages of a web project, the more important it becomes for inefficiency to be designed out from the very beginning.

Let's take a look at some of the ways good IA and UX can help improve sustainability.

Reduce unnecessary page loads

We saw in Chapter 2 that data transfer closely correlates with energy consumption. The more data the user loads, the more electricity needed to deliver that information to them and the more CO_2 emitted into the atmosphere.

The amount of data transferred is really determined by three things: the size of each page, the number of people visiting the site, and the number of pages each person visits on their journey through your site. It's this last point where IA and UX design can make the biggest impact.

With the average web page weighing in at nearly 2 MB, every page load consumes a lot of data, and with it, a significant amount of electricity (http://bkaprt.com/swd/01-06/). Every step in a user journey has a tangible impact on the environmental impact, and good structural design helps reduce that. Think about a hypothetical example. If a website user would typically visit three pages on their user journey, but you redesign the site so they can access the information they need by only visiting two pages, you'd significantly reduce the carbon footprint of their visit.

Furthermore, good IA and UX reduces friction for the user, and in the process reduces the amount of time it takes them to achieve their goal, whether it be to find a piece of information, sign up for an event, or buy new shoes. The longer a user stays on a website, the more electricity their device uses. Reducing wasted time by ensuring information is clearly structured helps to reduce emissions and create a better experience for the visitor.

The specific solutions will vary on a case-by-case basis, but here are a couple of common things to look out for that have a significant impact on energy consumption.

Long user journeys

Identify whether there are any long user journeys that seem to be common amongst your users. Look at where they start, finish, and pass through. Are the middle stages genuinely useful steps in the journey, or are you forcing users to pass through those pages to get to what they really want?

Gateway pages are often guilty of this. If you know you're looking for a small storage shelf on a furniture website, for example, do you really need to visit an intermediary landing page dedicated to staged photos of shelving solutions? More likely, you simply want to browse the catalog of actually available shelves. The British retail chain John Lewis & Partners resolves this inefficiency with a website that provides all specific subcategories in the dropdown menu when the user hovers over their preferred top-level category (**FIG 3.2**).

The experience is intuitive and leads the user quickly to their destination, with no need for in-between pages. They also include a prominent product search box to help users go straight to the product they're looking for.

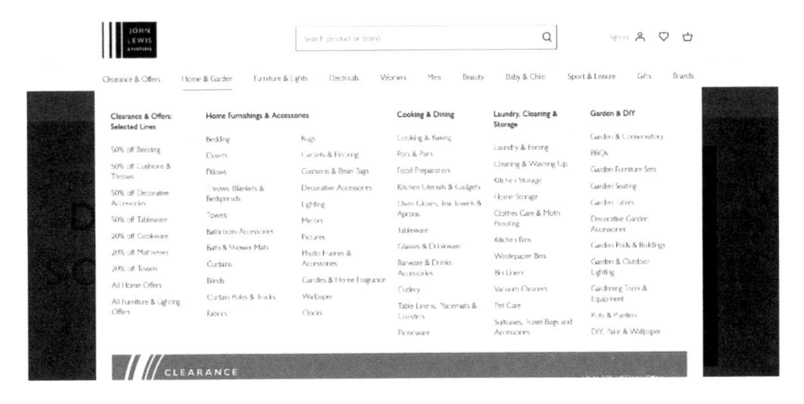

FIG 3.2: The John Lewis navigation menu eliminates the middle navigation level and simply offers users the full list of subcategories in the dropdown.

Yoyo user journeys

Another source of wasted page loads is the yoyo user journey, where a user keeps going into a page and back out of it—frequently the homepage. When you see this pattern, ask yourself why they keep going there. Are they getting lost, and the homepage is the only place that offers adequate orientation? Perhaps improving the navigation design so users feel confident to move between various areas of the website without returning to home will curtail this behavior.

Another example is often found on ecommerce websites, where users make several visits to the shopping cart throughout their journey. It may be that the user is reminding themselves what they've put in their cart or looking to see the total cost of what they've already added. This is an important requirement for the user and we want to make it as easy for them as possible. Finisterre does a great job of solving this with a shopping cart tab that slides in on the right side of the screen (**FIG 3.3**).

There is no separate cart page, as all of the content and functionality you would expect is provided in this neat little box. It also improves the user experience by allowing the shopper to seamlessly continue their journey through the site without losing their place when they check the cart.

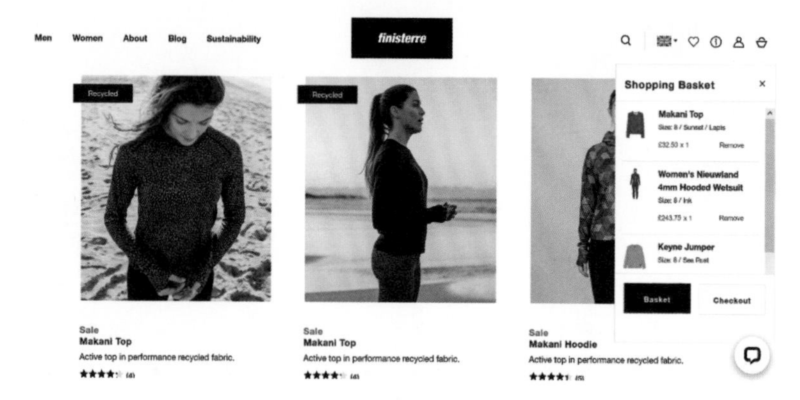

FIG 3.3: The Finisterre shopping basket appears on the right side of the screen as an overlay, eliminating the need for a separate cart page.

When users visit the same page multiple times, the amount of data loaded is significantly reduced on repeat visits. Therefore, the environmental impact of yoyoing visitors is not as large as other wasteful user journeys, but it does still have an impact, and designing to eliminate it can also deliver a better user experience.

Streamline the content

Amy Drayer is a user interface developer for the University of Minnesota Libraries. When the UML team came to migrate the Health Sciences Libraries (HSL) website from Drupal 7 to Drupal 8, they took the opportunity to do a redesign (http://bkaprt.com/swd/03-01/). Drayer told me she'd been thinking about a kind of "manifesto" for web designers and developers that became a pitch to the HSL team: to explore how *ethically* they could build the website.

This meant prioritizing accessibility, but also optimizing for sustainability. This ethical lens helped them streamline their content around a new set of design guidelines, which drastically reduced the number of words on each page, and reduced the page count from over three hundred to less than seventy—a reduction of roughly 75 percent! Drayer said the finished product wasn't only more energy-efficient, but also the most accessible website she had ever created.

We saw in the previous chapter that one source of wasted electricity in websites is the storage of data that's no longer needed. As websites grow over time, it's not uncommon for content to multiply. It's human nature that we're far more enthusiastic about creating new content than we are about cleaning out old content, just as we're more excited about buying new things than we are about cleaning out our cupboards.

But that old content isn't simply sitting there collecting dust; it's having a detrimental effect on the environment by filling up hard drives that consume electricity twenty-four hours a day, and it has a detrimental effect on visitors by making our website bloated, unwieldy, and confusing.

The problem is that content plans tend to be made in the process of creating a new website, and are too often forgotten once the excitement of launching the new website is over. But just because we forget doesn't mean the content plan is any less important. We need to continually return to it and review it in context of the changing needs of our users.

How do you know which pages aren't meeting your users' needs? One metric that can help shed some light on this is *bounce rate*.

Bounce rate: Are you meeting user expectations?

When people come to a website from an external source and they leave without visiting any other pages, we refer to this as a *bounce*. Although a high bounce rate is generally considered to be a bad thing, it very much depends on the user's motive for bouncing. A high bounce rate can be good if it means users quickly found exactly what they were looking for on the first page they visited, and therefore didn't feel the need to load any other pages. This means an effortless and satisfying experience for the user, and it's a win for the environment because it means they aren't loading additional pages unnecessarily.

On the other hand, if people bounce off your web page because they didn't like what they saw or find what they were hoping to, it means the page has failed to serve the user.

In a talk given to Wholegrain Digital, tech creative and STRADT consultant Brendan Roche compares this kind of bounce rate to something called *bycatch* in the fishing industry (http://bkaprt.com/swd/03-02/). Bycatch is where a fishing trawler catches a lot of fish that aren't commercially valuable, which are often then thrown back into the sea, dead, simply because the fishing nets have no way to distinguish which fish they actually catch. It's wasteful in the same way loading a website you never needed to visit in the first place is wasteful.

This is why a high bounce rate might indicate at least one of a few issues:

- Our content is structured in such a way that it attracts users looking for something different, which means we need to restructure our content to ensure both humans and search engines are clear about what we have to offer.
- We *are* attracting the right users to our website, but when they arrive, they cannot see what they were expecting to find. It's there somewhere, but the user experience we present to them obscures the key information they want, and so they leave unfulfilled.
- The content is so slow to load that users get frustrated and leave before the page has fully loaded.

The point is that bounce rate is not inherently good or bad—it all depends on why people are bouncing. Good IA and UX design ensure that any visitors who do bounce from our site do so for the right reasons. If we focus on the needs of our users and deliver what they want in a clear, simple, and intuitive structure, we save them time and reduce the number of pages they need to visit, saving energy and reducing emissions in the process.

We should adopt a holistic content management process where we phase out redundant content as we create new content, and regularly review the information architecture and user experience to ensure it still joins up in frictionless user journeys. We could do this by scheduling regular content audits and assigning time to content maintenance, just like we do for technical maintenance of our websites.

LIGHTWEIGHT IMAGERY

If you focus on just one thing when designing websites for sustainability, using images more efficiently has significant payoff. Don't get me wrong, when designing for the web, images can be critical to telling a story and making a strong visual impression, but they are one of the biggest contributors to carbon emissions on most websites.

According to HTTP Archive, the median number of images on any webpage is approximately thirty, with a total transfer size of 1 MB—equivalent to one hundred fifty thousand words of lorem ipsum in an HTML file (http://bkaprt.com/swd/03-03/). That's more than four times the length of this book! Even if a picture does speak a thousand words, it's still far less efficient than text.

We therefore need to think carefully about our use of images on the web. Like everything, we first need to question what value each image in our designs actually brings. Does it help the user to understand something, or is it critical to making the user experience enjoyable? Often the answer is yes, but in the case of stock photography, the answer is probably more commonly no. What is the user really gaining from that photo of a team of twenty-somethings pointing their fingers at a fake graph?

File size

If we must use images, we can reduce their weight by using the most efficient file formats and compression tools to optimize them.

- As a general rule, WEBP is the most efficient format for photographs, typically with files about 30 percent smaller than JPEG (http://bkaprt.com/swd/03-04/).
- AVIF, a newer image format, is quickly catching momentum in terms of browser compatibility, and can be less than half the size of WEBP (http://bkaprt.com/swd/03-05/).
- PNG or GIF are usually the most efficient formats for simple images that only use a few block colors, such as icons and logos.

- For video, MP4 is generally more efficient and delivers smaller files than animated GIF, and also provides better accessibility with features such as audio description tracks and captioning.

Even if you've used the most appropriate file format, it's likely the image or video file is bigger than it needs to be. Image compression tools like Shortpixel, TinyPNG and ImageOptim minimize file sizes without unwanted degradation of image quality (**FIG 3.4**). Many of these systems offer ways to integrate the tooling into your website so that all images are automatically optimized, which saves you time, reduces human error, and also compresses any autogenerated images (such as thumbnails) within your website.

You can actually reduce PNG file sizes even further if you take the time to optimize them by hand before you run them through a compression tool. There are over 16 million color channels in 24-bit PNG files, all of which are present in the file even if most of those colors are not used. Tools like ImageAlpha allow you to apply lossy compression and convert 24-bit PNG files to a more efficient PNG-8 files that include only the color channels needed. If you're using a PNG for a logo or icon that uses only a few block colors, this dramatically reduces the size of the file with no visible difference. In practice, if your image has more colors than can be displayed in a PNG-8 file, you would almost always be better off using a JPEG or WEBP format.

Another factor to consider is the dimensions at which the image is served. It's incredible how often images displayed as tiny thumbnails on the page are actually loaded as files big enough to fill an entire screen. Image file size roughly follows a square law, meaning that when you double the width and height, you more than double the file size. Therefore, loading unnecessarily large images has a disproportionate effect.

In the responsive web, images will be displayed at different sizes on different devices, so rather than uploading every image at the exact size in which it will be displayed, we generate multiple versions to suit different layouts. We can then use the `srcset` and `sizes` attributes in responsive markup to help

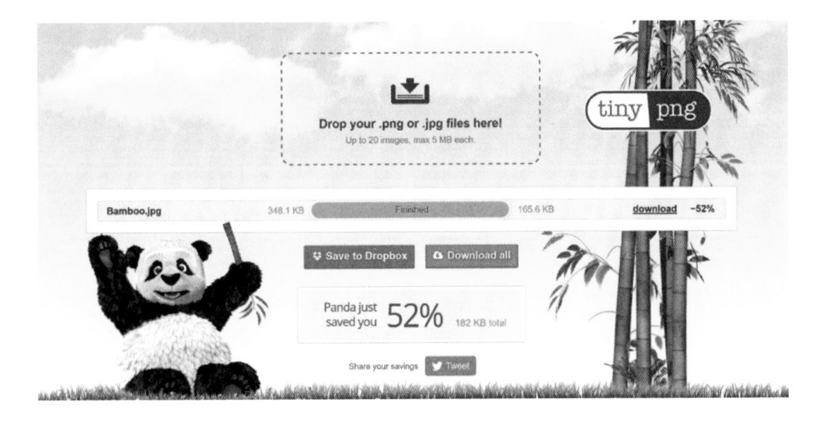

FIG 3.4: Tiny PNG significantly reduces file sizes with minimal hassle, and it has a cute panda. What's not to like?

inform browsers which image to load. This can lead to significant savings in data transfer, but the question of how many different variations to account for remains, since each one we provide as an option is another image that needs to be stored on a server, which itself uses energy and hardware.

The simplest approach is to make your best estimate for the most common viewport sizes your users will need, which should minimize the browser-side resizing. There is no perfect solution for configuring responsive image sizing to reduce energy consumption, but making optimal use of the existing tools inside most browsers today will get you a long way.

Blurring photographs

Image size is highly related to detail, so simple, clean imagery without a lot of intricate detail will deliver smaller image sizes. In the case of JPEG images in particular, blurring images can help make file sizes smaller because it reduces the amount of variation between each pixel. Of course, we don't want to blur the main subject of our images, but by using a shallow depth of field when taking photos, or by blurring out the edges of

FIG 3.5: The photo on the right is 47 percent smaller than the one on the left, simply because the edges are blurred.

images in editing before we upload them to our websites, we make images significantly smaller.

Una Kravets blew my mind in her talk "The Joy of Optimizing Images" when she demonstrated how a photograph of a mountain range could be nearly halved in size by blurring the foreground, with almost no noticeable difference to the viewer (http://bkaprt.com/swd/03-06/). I've done the same thing with a photo of a horse, which also reduced the image size by roughly half (**FIG 3.5**).

Vector imagery

We should also ask whether we can achieve the same or greater impact using other forms of styling instead of leaning on photographs. For example, can we create ambiance and strong brand experience with CSS styles? Can we use lightweight SVG vector files to illustrate ideas? Wherever we're using images, we should challenge ourselves to imagine what alternatives exist.

When we designed the website for children's charity Rights4Children, we needed to ensure the content was visually engaging for the children it serves, and could be accessed with minimal data usage, as these children live in institutional care and have limited access to the web. We used colorful vector illustrations to strike the perfect balance of visual interest and efficiency (**FIG 3.6**).

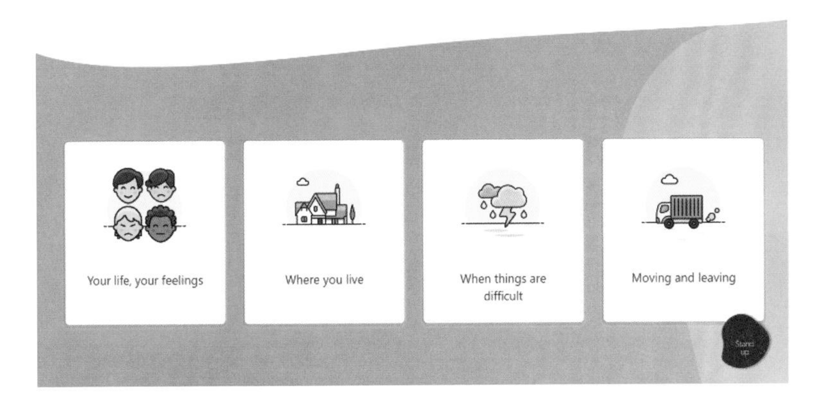

FIG 3.6: The children's rights website rights4children.org.uk uses SVG vector icons and vector background shapes to create visual interest with small file sizes.

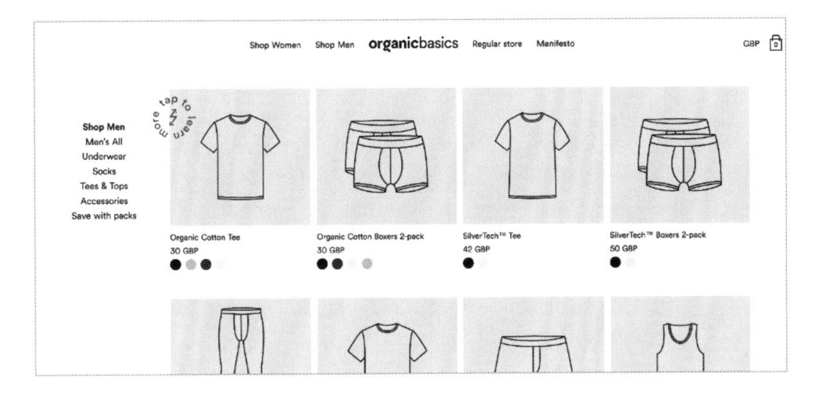

FIG 3.7: The low-impact website for Organic Basics embraces the simple idea that a t-shirt is just a t-shirt. What more do you need to know?

Clothing brand Organic Basics also uses vector imagery to great effect. They created a low-impact version of their website for users to browse instead of the regular version (**FIG 3.7**). On the low-impact website, all of the typical fashion photography is replaced with vector illustrations of the garments. It's a radical idea but it works, being beautiful, functional, and seven and a half times less data intensive than their standard website (http://bkaprt.com/swd/03-07/).

FIG 3.8: Smaller images with plenty of space make the critical messages stand out.

You can also manually optimize vector files before uploading them to a website. Using a vector editing software like Adobe Illustrator, you can delete any unused groups and layers in the file and simplify shapes by removing any unnecessary anchor points on paths. SVGs can also be edited in a code editor, albeit without the visual user interface. If there's anything you can delete without making any noticeable difference to the appearance of the image, then you have an opportunity to make the file smaller. On our team, we found that if we do manual optimizations first and *then* compress the SVG file using a tool like ImageOptim, we can reduce the size of vector files by up to 85 percent without anyone noticing.

Spacing

If we decide to use image files such as photographs, we still have a big opportunity to improve efficiency simply through careful sizing. Even a small reduction in width and height will greatly affect the file size without necessarily diminishing the visual impact. Pulling in the edges of an image and framing it with some space around it can actually make an image more impactful to the user while reducing the size of the image file itself. Clever use of space helps make content more engaging and accessible, reducing visual clutter and allowing our minds to process objects individually. Space can look great—and it's free.

THE COST OF COLOR

Color impacts the amount of energy used by a website in a couple of ways, as it can affect the amount of energy used by the user's screen, and it can impact the file size, too. Let's take a look at these two aspects of color.

Color and screen energy

If you're old enough to remember CRT monitors, you might also remember that dark websites were one of the first techniques popularized for saving energy. That idea quickly faded away with the advent of LCD flatscreens, which, unlike CRT monitors, have a permanent backlight, using the same energy regardless of the color visible on the screen.

However, most modern smart phones and a growing number of other devices such as laptops and smart TVs are now using OLED (*organic light-emitting diode*) screen technology that illuminates each pixel individually. As each pixel is literally a tiny LED, using darker colors is once again a viable technique to reduce energy on end-user devices. Google reported that the screen is the biggest single power draw on its phones and that for devices with OLED displays, darker colors make a significant difference (http://bkaprt.com/swd/03-08/):

- Running Google Maps in night mode reduced screen power draw by 63 percent.
- Black is the most efficient color for OLED screens as the pixels are switched off, and white is the most energy intensive, with darker colors generally using less energy.
- Color also makes a difference, with blue pixels consuming 25 percent more energy than green or red.

This isn't just good for the environment; it also helps to maximize battery life for portable devices such as phones, tablets, and laptops.

If you've been given some freedom as a designer to define the color palette for your branding, aim to create darker designs using less blue. When we updated the Wholegrain Digital brand

FIG 3.9: It was a bit of a facepalm moment when I realized we had the most energy intensive brand colors possible (left). We redesigned our brand identity to use more sustainable colors and to look more vibrant (right).

identity, we moved away from our previous color palette which was predominantly white with blue as the main accent color, and developed a darker, warmer palette that's not only lower energy but represents our brand better (FIG 3.9).

Color and file size

The second way in which color affects the energy used by a website is in its impact on the file size of images. As a general rule, the greater the amount of color variation in an image, the larger the file. Using images with reduced color variation is another way to curb a website's energy consumption.

Monochrome images generally produce smaller files than full color images. You might be wondering whether a black-and-white image would use more energy than a colored version due to it including more white, which as we have seen is the most energy intensive color on OLED screens. Potentially, this could be true, but there are a couple of reasons why grayscale or monochrome images will still tend to save energy over full color images. Firstly, reducing file sizes saves energy throughout the whole network—from the data center through the transmission network to the devices of all users—whereas the impact of screen energy only applies to end users with OLED screens. Secondly, although grayscale images can theoretically contain a lot of white, they can also contain a lot of black, which is the least energy intensive color, so to some extent the screen energy balances out.

Amy Drayer's ethical design system for the University of Minnesota Libraries didn't just lead to an overhaul of the website content, it permeated every decision on the project including the color of images. Drayer told me that the use of black-and-white images on the website was the single biggest sticking point with colleagues, but she had good support from the team and they made the decision to be bold and use only grayscale images. This significantly reduced file sizes, helping to make the website more sustainable and improving web performance.

If black-and-white images aren't your thing, don't rule out monochrome images just yet: monochrome images don't have to be black-and-white. We can get creative and apply color to

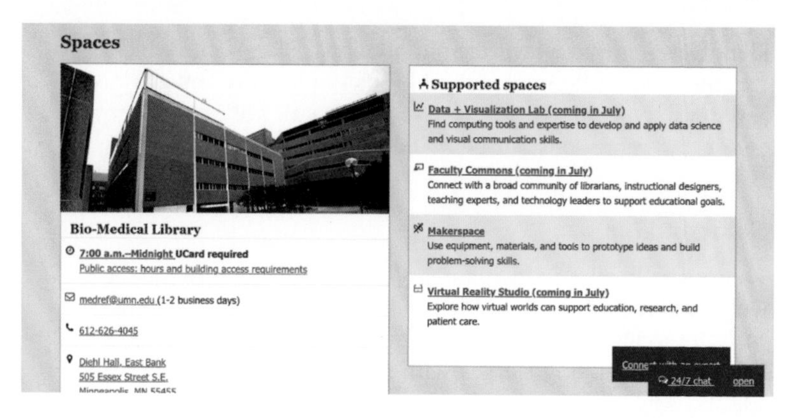

FIG 3.10: The University of Minnesota Bio-Medical Library team made a conscious choice to use black-and-white images to reduce file sizes on their website.

grayscale images, either in our photo editing software, or in the browser using CSS blend modes. This creates the appearance of color images while using smaller grayscale files.

Most browsers support blend modes such as color overlay, screen, and even gradients, but we should always make sure we use progressive enhancement so the original image is still displayed for users whose browsers don't support blend modes. We should also keep in mind that using CSS blend modes may cause a device to use more energy computing a change of color on the fly; in some cases, we may find that it's a false economy compared to just using a color image in the first place.

By experimenting with different blend modes and checking the impact on browser energy impact as we discussed in Chapter 2, you can find solutions that use small files and have minimal impact on browser energy. Keep in mind that CPU usage for overlay effects increases as the image is scaled to fill more of the screen, and will therefore rise with image size. If you have multiple overlay effects on the same page, it could result in very high CPU usage.

BE MINDFUL WITH MOTION

Motion brings the web to life. Used well, it helps us create better user experiences and communicate information more effectively but the benefits are not inherent. Used in the wrong way, motion can confuse and disorient users, make information less accessible, and use a lot of energy. This isn't just an environmental issue, but for portable device users, it can drain batteries faster, which is a real problem for people who are out and about without access to a power supply.

We must use motion mindfully if we are to create positive web experiences for all users and keep the environmental impact to a minimum. Other than using less motion in our designs, we can do put control into users' hands by way of the Reduced Motion Media Query, which can be implemented to turn off large aspects of movement for users who specify a preference for reduced motion in their System Preferences. Perhaps someday this same query could even be used to create a "low power mode" setting in browsers.

Web video

Images might be the biggest source of carbon emissions on most websites, but that's because most websites don't have videos—yet. For those that do have video, it will nearly always eclipse everything else on the website in terms of carbon emissions, as videos are both data and processing intensive.

Streaming video is one of the largest sources of internet emissions, and it's growing fast as we get accustomed to consuming more of our information and entertainment in video format. A study by the University of Bristol found that streaming videos from YouTube produces approximately 10 kg of CO_2 per hour, or 2.8 grams per second (http://bkaprt.com/swd/03-09/).

So, what can we do to minimize this? Obviously, the first step is to avoid videos if we don't need them. It's easy to assume that people want to consume content as video, but it's not always the case.

Joe Jones is the cofounder of design agency Archipelago and a digital content creator specializing in making complex topics easy to understand. He explained to me that while video has its place, we shouldn't assume it's always the best content format. Firstly, video generally has sound, which makes it awkward to view in public spaces such as the office or on public transport. You know that moment of panic as the web page you opened starts blasting sound across the office, broadcasting, "Look at me, I'm watching videos on work time!" Yep, we've all been there in the embarrassing scramble to find the mute button or close the tab. Secondly, the high bandwidth requirements of video make them slow to load on mobile connections, not to mention the fact that they burn through monthly data limits on mobile devices.

Jones also points out that videos give the user little control over the timeline, making it hard for people to browse at their own pace. With most web content, you can skim through it quickly and stop to study elements of particular interest to you. With video, you have to sit through it from beginning to end—turning users into passengers rather than drivers of their own experience.

Renewable heating supplier Nu Heat was looking for a visually engaging way to explain how heat pumps work and was considering producing an animated video to embed on their website. On reviewing the requirements, we found that interactive web animation would be a better solution, with accessible text, better mobile usability, the ability to click in and out of different stages of the process, and smaller file sizes (**FIG 3.11**). By adapting an After Effects animation for the web using Lottie, we were able to create an interactive animation in just 575 KB—far more efficient than the 13 MB we'd estimated for a well-optimized video offering the same information (http://bkaprt.com/swd/03-10/).

If you do decide that video is the best format for a particular piece of content, you can still take steps in design and content creation to reduce the environmental impact. The most powerful step is to think about how users interact with the videos. For example, avoid designs that involve autoplaying video, such as video backgrounds. Autoplay videos aren't only bad for the environment, they can also cause problems for users with sensory disorders and motion sensitivity. Putting a play button

How does a heat pump work?

1. EVAPORATOR 2. COMPRESSOR 3. CONDENSER 4. EXPANSION VALVE

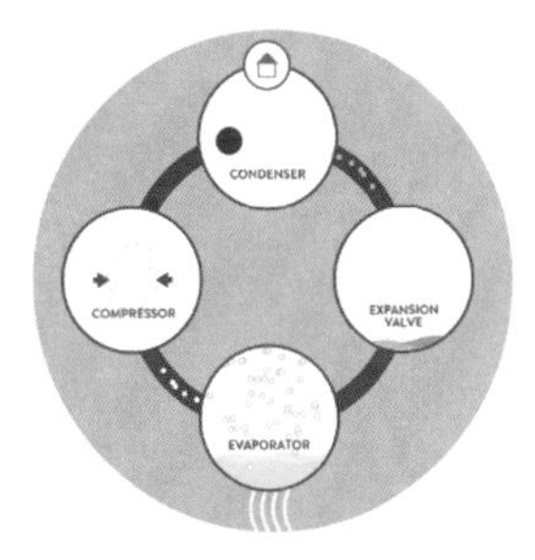

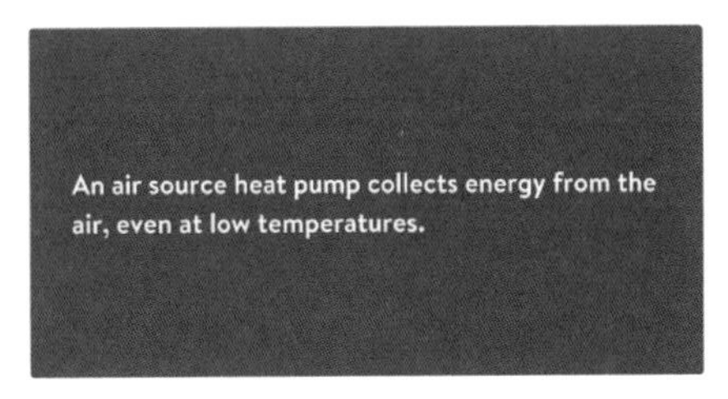

FIG 3.11: Nu Heat used an energy-saving interactive animation instead of a video to explain how energy saving heat pumps work (http://bkaprt.com/swd/03-11/).

in front of any video ensures it only loads if the user definitely wants to watch it, which is much better for user experience and significantly cuts down on unnecessary streaming of data.

You can also optimize video files to reduce the file size without losing any noticeable image quality. Neil Clark of digital agency Manifesto wrote a blog series about the environmental impact of digital, and included a video showing how he calculated the carbon emissions of a web page. The original video was 80 MB as a WEBM file, but after it was compressed as an MP4 file, it was only 3 MB. The video looked the same to the viewer but was less than 4 percent of the original size (http://bkaprt.com/swd/03-12/).

Content also plays an important role in the environmental impact of video, with the most important factor being length. With a single second of video content consuming more data than a single full screen JPEG image, every second really does count. We can save users time and help the environment by keeping it short and snappy.

GIF animations

GIF files have come back into fashion for sharing short animations, but, OMG, those memes come at a cost! Aside from their poor image quality, GIF animations are horrendously inefficient because they effectively save every frame as a separate GIF image and then merge them together into one big file. Think carefully before adding GIFs to any web page, and if you do need to use short animations in your designs, consider using a more efficient format. WEBP is a far more efficient image format that supports animation and in many cases it can be more efficient to instead use short videos, delivering higher picture quality with significantly smaller files.

Go easy on the icing

As designers of the modern web, we want to create experiences that feel dynamic and interactive, not flat and static. We want to add nice flourishes to our websites in the form of animated interactions, loading effects, hover or scroll effects, and other forms of motion and interest. This icing on the cake can make the difference between a website being "nice" and it being "delicious." The question is, what is the cost of using these effects?

Our team at Wholegrain Digital ran some tests while developing our own website and found that even "simple" effects can have a significant impact on the end users' CPU usage. For example, adding a carousel to an image gallery instead of displaying static images on the page increased peak CPU usage by 7 percent. Adding a simple fade-in effect on page load increased peak CPU usage by 22 percent. These figures will vary depending on the exact use case and the performance of the user's own device, but they nevertheless highlight how animations and interactions that feel effortless to the user may in fact require a lot of effort from the user's device. In addition to the environmental impact, this can also be a pain for people using portable devices, as it will drain their battery faster.

That's not to say we should give people a bare sponge cake with no icing at all. We must find a delicate balance between effects that genuinely improve the user experience and support the core purpose of the website, and those that are just a bit too gluttonous.

We must ask ourselves what purpose our animations and interactions really serve and whether simple, more lightweight alternatives are available. Work with developers to test the energy impact and file sizes of the proposed effects to inform your decisions. The perfect design will not feel like a compromise. It will deliver enough to feel great, and nothing more.

EFFICIENT WEB TYPOGRAPHY

Commercial and open-source webfonts have vastly expanded the typographic options available to designers, but they can also take a heavy environmental toll by increasing data transfer and the number of server requests required to load a page. As designers, we should think carefully about which typefaces we choose, and what the implications might be for our page weight budget.

The most efficient choice is always to use system fonts that come pre-installed on devices, such as Arial, Times New Roman, or Helvetica on Apple devices, and Roboto on Android. System fonts require zero server requests and zero data transfer to use. They are essentially free. The downside is that they restrict creative freedom, and because they're not the same on every device, you sacrifice some level of control over presentation.

When you do use high-impact non-system fonts, it helps to be strategic. Headings and menus, for example, tend to command much more visual weight than body text, so an eye-catching font is likely to have more impact there; users may not even notice you then use system fonts for the body copy.

Other key considerations include whether your preferred typeface is available as a standalone webfont whose files you host directly, or if it's licensed via a subscription font service such as Adobe Fonts or Fonts.com. These subscription services can add extra weight to your website and make additional server requests, increasing energy consumption and slowing your site down, while also limiting the extent to which web developers can optimize the fonts, as we'll see later. The good thing about

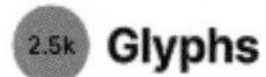

Inter Regular Sample

ABCDEFGHIJKLMN
OPQRSTUVWXYZ
abcdefghijklmnopq
rstuvwxyz () & ?! @
1234567890 .,:; /→

Inter Bold Sample

ABCDEFGG

FIG 3.12: The open-source typeface Inter UI is comprehensive, with over two thousand characters and eighteen styles, but most websites don't need all of them (http://bkaprt.com/swd/03-13/).

subscription fonts is knowing your fonts are legally licensed, but from an efficiency standpoint, you'll probably want to avoid subscription fonts where possible and host your own. Just be aware that the licenses on some fonts do limit modifications, so you'll need to check the legal terms yourself before making changes to the files.

The next consideration from a design perspective is how many different fonts and weights are needed (**FIG 3.12**). Generally, each weight comes as a separate font file, adding bulk to the page. Do you really need standard, light, semi-bold, bold, *and* black? Probably not.

Reducing the number of font files makes pages faster and cleaner, and helps make your designs more consistent. In cases where your project genuinely does need a wide variety of font styles, consider using a variable font. Variable fonts are designed to allow precise scaling of thickness and slant, allowing infinite variations of a single typeface to be rendered from a single font file. It's a highly efficient solution, and the main downside is the limited number of variable fonts currently available. A good place to start is Variable Fonts, a project to help designers and developers become more familiar with OpenType variable fonts (http://bkaprt.com/swd/03-14/).

DESIGNING A SUSTAINABLE FUTURE

When we embrace the spirit of minimalism, not just from an aesthetic perspective, but also from an efficiency perspective, we can achieve more with less.

By questioning every detail and thinking critically about how we might create better solutions, not only can we reduce the emissions of the products we design, but we can also make them more effective for users and for businesses.

Now that we've learned how design decisions impact the energy demanded by a digital product, let's learn more about the technical approaches we can take to delivering a sustainable web.

4 SUSTAINABLE WEB DEVELOPMENT

ASIDE FROM THE GENERAL BENEFITS of reliability, security, and maintainability, well-written code is inherently more efficient. If you can write in ten lines of code what you used to write in a hundred lines, you've not only reduced the size of the file, but likely reduced the amount of work the server has to do to process that file.

Think about the way you write code from a structural point of view. Can you organize your files to be more streamlined and avoid duplication of styles and functions? Can you simplify logic to reduce the number and complexity of queries required to deliver a specific piece of functionality? Can you code the website without using bloated libraries and plugins that contain functionality you don't even need? It might take a bit more time to plan an efficient structure or to write code from scratch, but the benefits in terms of performance and sustainability can be significant.

Of course, we live in a reality where time is short. Hand-coding everything might deliver technical efficiency, but might not be a good use of our own time. Likewise, we might not have the experience or confidence to code everything from scratch.

We don't need to be dogmatic about it, but we do need to commit to making informed decisions about our solutions. Even if we need to use an off-the-shelf option, a little research could reveal a more appropriate and less bloated solution.

Let's drop the assumption that because developers' time is more expensive than computer time, computing efficiency is not worth pursuing. According to Nikita Prokopov, this attitude in our industry results in us "wasting computers at an unprecedented scale" (http://bkaprt.com/swd/04-01/). It reminds me of something Guy Singh-Watson, founder of Riverford Organic Farms, wrote in one of his veg box newsletters: "Until energy is more expensive, I suspect we will keep thinking of new ways to waste it" (http://bkaprt.com/swd/04-02/). We must start valuing energy and natural resources as much as we value our own time and effort.

ENERGY EFFICIENT LANGUAGES

If efficient code helps us create more sustainable web services, it's worth asking what difference programming languages themselves make to the energy efficiency.

A team of six researchers from Portuguese universities set out to investigate exactly that (http://bkaprt.com/swd/04-03/, PDF). They ran server energy tests of twenty-seven popular programming languages, using ten standardized algorithmic problems from a free software project called the Computer Language Benchmarks Game (http://bkaprt.com/swd/04-04/).

They found the energy efficiency of different languages varies significantly, and although the results varied by context, there was a clear pattern that compiled languages delivered the highest levels of energy efficiency (**FIG 4.1**): "On average, compiled languages consumed 120 J [joules] to execute the solutions, while for a virtual machine and interpreted languages this value was 576 J and 2365 J, respectively." Those are some profound differences! (The notable exception to this rule was Java, which came in at just 114 joules.)

The researchers found that the three least energy intensive programming languages were C, Rust, and C++, while the three

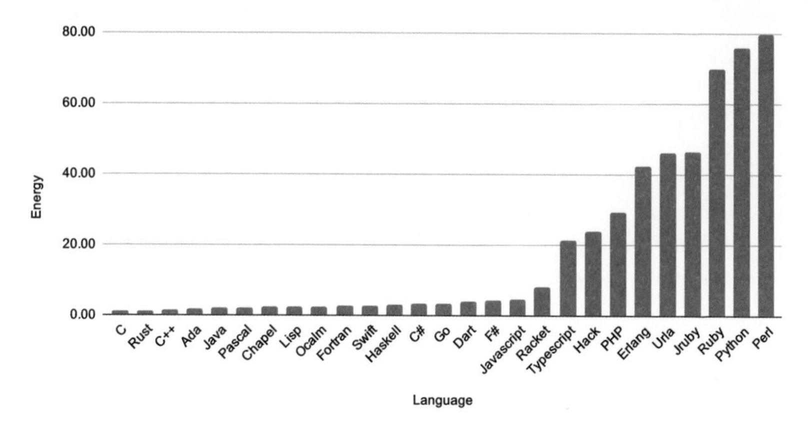

FIG 4.1: The variation in energy efficiency of programming languages is astonishing.

most energy intensive were Perl, Python, and Ruby. Popular web programming languages JavaScript and PHP ranked 17th and 21st respectively, which is a little troubling when we consider these languages power the majority of modern websites. Some small consolation was that JavaScript and PHP were two of the most energy efficient languages when manipulating strings with regular expression, even though "they tend to be not very energy efficient in other scenarios," according to the report.

When looking at actual energy consumption (rather than ranking), JavaScript is far more efficient than PHP or Ruby, using just 4.4 joules to complete an average task, compared to 29.3 joules for PHP and 69.9 joules for Ruby. In other words, JavaScript uses 15 percent of the energy of PHP and just 6.3 percent of that consumed by Ruby.

In practice, we have to use programming languages appropriate to the project and with which we have sufficient proficiency to deliver our work, but knowing which languages are most efficient helps us decide which languages to use in those cases where we *do* have a choice. It also provides guidance to help us intentionally choose which programming languages to learn and use in the future.

Use JavaScript with care

Despite the comparative benefits of JavaScript, I'm going to single it out as a language we should try to use less. I know what you're thinking; "This guy isn't making any sense!"

Let me explain. Although JavaScript might be more energy efficient in processing algorithmic problems, it will always be less efficient than serving static files in cases where we don't need our code to "solve problems."

The most common example is the use of JavaScript for animating elements in a web design. CSS can now achieve many animation effects with far more efficiency than JavaScript because it minimizes the need for the CPU to "think"—and can generally be achieved with far smaller file sizes, minimizing the energy used to transfer data.

We should think carefully about whether the code we use is necessary. For example, does our website really need jQuery to deliver the functionality specified, and is it appropriate to use a front-end framework like React, Vue, or Angular for simple websites that don't have any need for them?

Likewise, the functionality that JavaScript adds tends to consume energy and slow websites down, without contributing value for the user. And that brings me to tracking scripts.

Tracking scripts

One of the most common uses of JavaScript is for advertising and tracking scripts, which are at best a distraction and in many cases an invasion of privacy.

Simple analytics tracking scripts vary enormously in size. The standard Google Analytics script runs 17 KB, while Google Tag Manager is significantly heavier at 75 KB; more streamlined options are a fraction of that at 1.5 KB for Minimal GA and 1.2 KB for Fathom at the time of writing (http://bkaprt.com/swd/04-05/). It's worth questioning what functionality you need from your tracking script to justify the extra weight.

News websites are notorious for having an excess of tracking and advertising scripts. In 2015, the *New York Times* reviewed the data consumption of fifty popular news websites and found that, on average, over half of the data consumption came solely from advertising scripts. In addition to causing significant performance issues, these scripts end up costing mobile users a large chunk of their monthly data allotments. A user could spend up to thirty-two cents of a typical data plan loading just the ads on a news homepage—while the editorial content would cost only eight cents (http://bkaprt.com/swd/04-06/).

Tracking scripts can undo a lot of our great work in creating an efficient website. To solve this, we need to be less passive about simply installing all the scripts requested by the marketing department at the end of the design and development process, and engage in an open conversation about what exactly we are trying to learn from the data. There may be much smaller tracking scripts that can provide the data we actually need.

We can also reduce the impact of tracking scripts by asking *when* they are needed. We may not need to use tracking scripts indefinitely, but instead could install them temporarily to track a campaign or understand a specific UX problem, and then remove them once we have the necessary insights.

We might not always have full control over what tracking scripts end up on the websites we create, but by asking the right questions and proactively suggesting more efficient alternatives, we can help steer things in the right direction.

OPTIMIZING FONT FILES

When we decided to use Inter UI as the typeface on the Wholegrain Digital website, we were concerned that a single font weight came standard as a 298 KB TTF file—larger than the rest of the front-end code put together. So we investigated how we could reduce the size. We started with the original Inter UI font file in TTF format and converted it to a more efficient WOFF2 file format using Font Squirrel's Webfont Generator (**FIG 4.2**) (http://bkaprt.com/swd/04-07/). This reduced the file size to 77 KB with no loss of quality whatsoever.

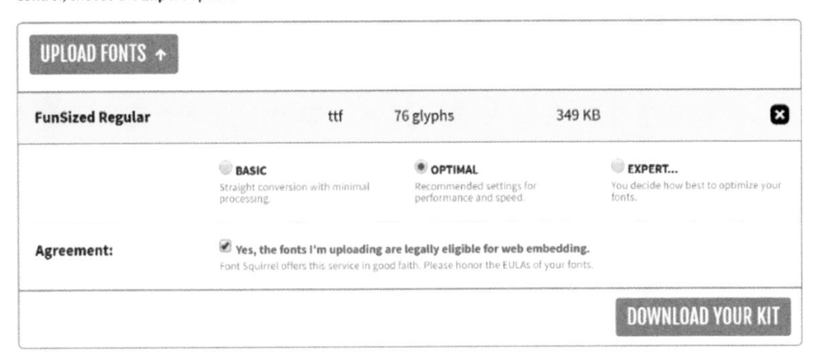

FIG 4.2: It seems all the best tools are run by cute animals. Font Squirrel's Webfont Generator is a simple way to convert fonts to the optimal format in no time.

The next question was whether the font included any elements we didn't need. Using the character map viewer provided by Font Drop, we were able to see that our Inter UI font file contained 2,192 characters supporting thirty-nine languages, most of which our website simply didn't need (http://bkaprt.com/swd/04-08/). We used the font subsetting tool from Everything Fonts to strip out the unused characters, leaving us with a subsetted version of Inter UI containing only ninety-eight characters (http://bkaprt.com/swd/04-09/). The final file was a mere 7 KB, a reduction of 97.7 percent in file size compared to the official Inter UI file we'd started with, and without any negative side effects for users of our website.

So long as you have control of the font files, and the foundry's license terms allow for web use and optimization, you can repeat this process for almost any font, improving performance and sustainability with just a few minutes of effort.

STAYING STATIC

If you were born before 1990, you'll probably remember the days when we used to build websites in static HTML, and when we made our dreams come true with Dreamweaver. It turns out that those basic websites were really, really ecofriendly because they generally had really small files and placed minimal load on the server.

The interaction between the browser and the server amounted to something like this:

Browser: "Can I have the homepage?"
Server: "Sure, here it is."

With the introduction of content management systems (CMSes), that process has become a lot more complicated. The actual HTML files no longer exist on the web server; the server has to generate the files every time someone requests the web page. Think of old-fashioned static HTML web pages as microwave-ready meals, while CMS-based web pages are raw ingredients that need chopping and cooking before anyone can eat them. Despite the incredible power CMSes have given us to take control of our content, the technology enabling this control is a lot less efficient, resulting in higher energy consumption and slower load times.

It's difficult to put a number on exactly how much extra energy this uses, but we can get an indication by comparing the amount of computation required to load a simple HTML file to the same content from a PHP file (used by popular CMSes like WordPress and Drupal).

At the Web Performance for People and Planet event held in London in 2019, the CTO of the Positive Internet Company, Nick Mailer, gave a presentation in which he suggested using the number of system calls on the server as an indicator of the relative amount of energy used to load a file. He created a static HTML file and an equivalent PHP script to deliver the exact same content to the browser: the string "hello, world." The static file used forty-six system calls, while the PHP file used

888 system calls—nearly twenty times the amount of work on the server.

Fortunately, solutions exist that can reduce the number of system calls on the server. Let's take a look at some of them.

Page caching

One common solution is page caching, where most of the page is generated on the fly by the CMS when the first visitor loads the page, and all subsequent visits receive a cached version of the page. Although the server still has to do the resource-intensive work of generating and populating the markup for the first visitor to a new or updated page, every subsequent visitor to that page will receive that same generated copy of the page's HTML.

This not only saves a lot of computational energy, it also greatly improves web performance, because the user doesn't need to wait for the page to be "assembled" on the server before it can be sent to their browser.

A plugin like WP Rocket is the easiest way to implement caching in a CMS such as WordPress. WP Rocket generates the cached version of our web pages for us, and can also pregenerate the cache by simulating the first visit. This helps us avoid slow load times for the first visitor to each newly edited page, and also helps search engine rankings by ensuring all pages are cached *before* the search engine crawler visit.

However, when we implement a caching solution inside our CMS, the CMS itself still has to fire up and process every request before sending the static files to the visitor. We can eliminate this initial overhead by moving the caching layer onto the hosting itself. The server sends the cached files directly to the user without querying the CMS, saving energy and improving load times even further. Server-side caching technologies like Varnish are widely available and come standard in some hosting packages, so even if you don't have the technical knowledge to set caching up yourself, you can still apply it to your projects.

Page caching also increases resilience to traffic spikes. For example, one of our client's sites had a million and a half hits inside a week from bots trolling their traffic. The server held up just fine because it didn't have to do any of that heavy Word-Press stuff. To quote my colleague Josh Stopper, it was like the server just said, "Here's the traffic. Here's the file. Bye." Job done!

JAMstack

Caching isn't the only solution for eliminating the inefficiency caused by content management systems dynamically generating web pages. An emerging approach that can help us create a more sustainable web is the *JAMstack*.

JAMstack might sound like something you would eat for breakfast, but it actually stands for *JavaScript, APIs, and Markup*. By using the growing power of JavaScript in modern web browsers, combined with APIs that can interact with other web services, JAMstack is a way to decouple the CMS from the front-end user experience.

A JAMstack website uses a content management system to edit and publish content, and then the web pages themselves prerender as static web pages. This approach delivers the performance, security, and energy efficiency of purely static web pages—and unlike the static websites of the early web, it can also deliver the rich interactions, advanced functionality, and CMS-based content editing we expect from the modern web. JAMstack websites typically also host the static files on a content delivery network (CDN), saving energy by reducing the distance files have to travel to each visitor and creating resilience by eliminating any single point of failure.

It's an approach rather than a technology, but it's becoming ever more accessible to apply to our projects. There are a growing number of JAMstack frameworks and content management systems, such as Jekyll, Netlify, Hugo, and Gatsby.

This approach is similar to hosting services (such as Strattic and Shifter) that do the hard work of converting our preferred content management systems into static websites. When people visit these websites, they are hitting static web pages with no connection to the CMS. In fact, the CMS doesn't even exist unless the editor is logged in and editing content. So-called "serverless" hosting solutions are designed so that when the user logs in, it spins up a live version of the CMS, generates static files for the web pages, and then winds down the CMS again when the website editor logs out.

This makes perfect sense. Web-based CMSes are extremely useful for empowering people to publish and manage content on the web, but if visitors are being served static files from a CDN, then there's no need for the CMS to be running on a server and using electricity unless someone is actually logged into the CMS editing the website.

Josh Lawrence, cofounder of serverless WordPress host Strattic, told me that, although it's hard to obtain exact numbers, a static implementation of WordPress is likely to use several hundred times less energy than using WordPress in its default form.

As for whether the JAMstack approach is more efficient than a well cached conventional CMS website, that's a matter of debate. The difference is marginal if you've set up your CMS to get everything working efficiently. The key difference is JAMstack has the efficiency benefits of static websites by default, whereas with conventional content management systems you have to pay attention to detail to ensure it's all set up to perform efficiently, which is often not the case.

Progressive Web Apps

Progressive Web App (PWA) technology is a close ally of static web technology—it helps us develop more efficient websites by bringing many of the features previously unique to native mobile apps into the web browser. PWAs are now supported in most web browsers, and offer numerous benefits in terms of user experience, such as the ability to cache files on a user's device with a high degree of control.

Carefully designed caching reduces the number of times the browser makes requests to the server, as well as the amount of data transfer. This is particularly effective on pages that users are likely to visit multiple times but don't change very often, such as reference articles. In addition to benefiting the environment, it also improves load speeds and makes websites seem more stable when the web connection is a bit flaky, such as when commuting on the train—not to mention providing resilience during natural disasters when telecoms networks are often compromised.

In *Progressive Web Apps*, Jason Grigsby argued that there really is no good reason for any website not to harness the benefits of PWAs: "Even if you don't think of your website as an 'app,' the core features of progressive web apps can benefit any website. Who wouldn't profit from a fast, secure, and reliable website?" Add "energy-efficient" to that list!

COMPRESS YOUR CODE

Having written your super-clean, well-organized code, there's one more thing to do before you upload it to your hosting account and call it a day: compression!

No matter how well you write your code, it can always be more streamlined. As humans, we like certain "niceties" in code that machines don't care about: white space for legibility, comments to help us understand it, and intuitive naming of classes and functions. What's more, we're not perfect, and will often include some unused or duplicated code.

While these extras are fine in the development process, they make our files larger than they need to be. If we can strip them out of our work and generate a version of our code that's purely machine-readable, then we can save energy and improve web performance.

Build tools help us do this by converting the development code we read and write as humans into a production-ready version optimized for machines. Build tools can be used for many things, including checking code against web standards and browser compatibility, but it's their ability to compress code that we're interested in here.

It can be complicated to set up build tools because there's a different tool for every optimization we want to apply. CodeKit is a piece of software written for people fed up with managing multiple open-source tools to produce a website build (http://bkaprt.com/swd/04-10/). It will take pretty much any code you give it, run it through build tools, and compile it into the most efficient format. It works with images, JavaScript, CSS, PHP, almost anything you like. It doesn't have all of the flexibility you'd get from setting up custom build tools, but as a starting point, it's powerful.

BLOCK THE BOTS

Having spent most of this chapter explaining ways you can make your code more efficient, there's one really easy way you can reduce the environmental impact of your websites with minimal effort.

In one word—bots!

As web designers we're very much focused on creating products that serve the needs of the user—but human users aren't the only ones visiting our websites. A huge percentage of website traffic comes from bots.

Bots visit websites for a wide variety of reasons—web scrapers, SEO bots like Ahrefs and SEMRush, brute force attackers trying to break in, RSS reader apps, competitors monitoring each other's websites, and "script kiddies" just playing with bots.

Akshat Choudhary, founder of the WordPress backup and security service BlogVault, told me that their data shows "bots often use up 50 percent of resources such as processing and bandwidth. We observe this consistently across all sites."

Remember that I mentioned in Chapter 1 that if the internet were a country, it would be equal to Germany as the sixth worst polluter in the world? Now imagine if 50 percent of Germany's electricity was being siphoned off by bots that are up to no good. Surely it would be a national priority to keep the bots out.

This is how we should be thinking about bots in our web projects. We might not see them, but they're there, trying to extract information and breach our security. In the process, they put additional load on our servers and slow down our websites.

We need to keep the bots out, and luckily, in many cases, it's not too difficult. Bots can be blocked primarily by using a firewall, which can be added to most websites using a service such as Cloudflare or Malcare, or by your hosting provider.

These services will block the majority of bots, but still let in the ones you want (hello, Google!).

With this in place, you can not only reduce the carbon footprint of your website, you can also improve load speeds, enhance security, and stop competitors from scraping your information. Win!

BETTER, MORE SUSTAINABLE CODE

The bottom line when developing websites and apps is that it's important to remember just how much influence you have over the sustainability of the end product, regardless of whether or not you were involved in the design process. A thoughtful, detail-oriented approach to development leads to websites that are far more efficient without any perceivable difference to the user other than improved performance. That's a pretty good side effect.

No matter what type of web project you work on or what coding technologies you use, one thing is certain—it will need to be hosted somewhere, and we're talking about that next.

5 GREEN WEB HOSTING

ONE OF THE MOST EFFICIENT websites we've tested through the Website Carbon Calculator is the personal website of David and Kay Cawsey (**FIG 5.1**). Their simple blog doesn't live on a server in a big data center in Dallas or London. It lives on a Raspberry Pi in the back of their cupboard in Cheltenham, England.

Davidandkay.me.uk might not be an all-singing, all-dancing, modern web application, but it highlights another option available to achieve hosting efficiency. David's approach bypasses the need for complex server technology by keeping things simple and efficient. "A simple server does not need an entire 'LAMP STACK'," he explains on his site. "Apache is a bit 'heavyweight.'"

You see, David isn't like most of us modern web designers who have grown up with a mindset of abundance. David is eighty-seven years old and has been working with computers since the early 1950s—so most of his career has required a lightweight approach:

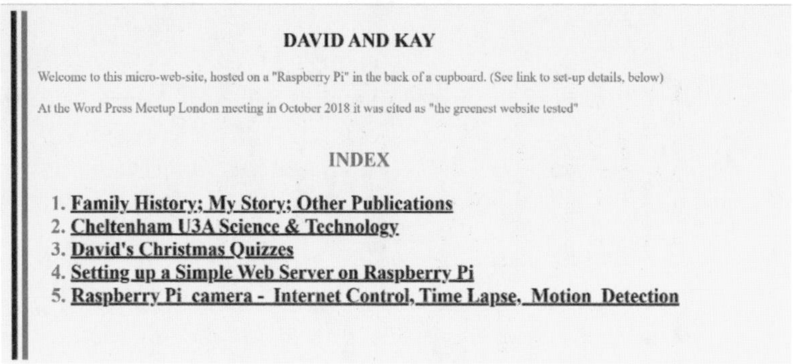

DAVID AND KAY

Welcome to this micro-web-site, hosted on a "Raspberry Pi" in the back of a cupboard. (See link to set-up details, below)

At the Word Press Meetup London meeting in October 2018 it was cited as "the greenest website tested"

INDEX

1. Family History; My Story; Other Publications
2. Cheltenham U3A Science & Technology
3. David's Christmas Quizzes
4. Setting up a Simple Web Server on Raspberry Pi
5. Raspberry Pi camera - Internet Control, Time Lapse, Motion Detection

FIG 5.1: It might not be flashy, but there's a lot we can learn here!

> *[I] had to be efficient, with slow processors and very limited memory. The Internet arrived in the 1990s, and for many years we used dial-up, with slow (56 KBps) modems. I soon did some websites, commercially hosted, and it was certainly good practice to keep them simple and minimize file sizes. That's stayed with me, and it's against my frugal nature to include graphics files which are unnecessarily huge or use code which I don't understand!*

David has lived in a world where computing power and the speed of data networks was limited in a way most of us would now struggle to comprehend, so he intuitively understands the value of being efficient. It's a lesson in valuing resources and keeping things simple—easy to forget in a world of cheap and abundant processing power and super-fast internet.

We consume data as if it's the air we breathe. In contrast with David's website on his Raspberry Pi, the average website is now so big it wouldn't even fit on a floppy disk (if you remember those!). As our society consumes more and more data, energy-hungry data centers are multiplying like mice, at great expense to the environment.

THE COST OF DATA

Data centers are one of the fastest growing sources of electricity demand globally, and with much of the world's energy still produced by burning fossil fuels, they present a genuine threat to our chances of meeting the Paris Agreement goals.

In 2015 I interviewed Fabio Torlini, the EMEA managing director of hosting company WP Engine, for our Wholesome Business podcast. He told me that a typical data center uses roughly as much electricity as Maidenhead in England, a town that's home to over sixty thousand people. That's just *one* data center. All of that electricity production, much of it from coal- and gas-fired power stations, is a major contributor to climate change.

On top of that, our hunger for data is growing as we move more of our lives online and create more data-intensive web services. According to a report by researchers Anders Andrae and Tomas Edler, "data centers will use around 3–13% of global electricity in 2030 compared to 1% in 2010" (**FIG 5.2**) (http://bkaprt.com/swd/05-01/).

This is why it's so important we use hosting efficiently, and rapidly move to ensure all data centers, large and small, are powered by renewable energy.

The server room

It wasn't so long ago that many businesses had their own server rooms full of computers running IT systems. If you ever went into one of these rooms, you'll remember how hot and stuffy they were. Computers operate most efficiently when they're cool, and they give off a lot of heat when in use. When you pack a bunch of them together in one room, things start to get pretty toasty, and it becomes necessary to cool the server rooms down in order to keep the machines running efficiently. This, in turn, uses more electricity to power the air conditioning.

It turns out the traditional office server room was highly inefficient, not to mention expensive to operate. They suffer from the curse of mediocrity, being neither big enough to achieve economies of scale nor small enough to enjoy the ben-

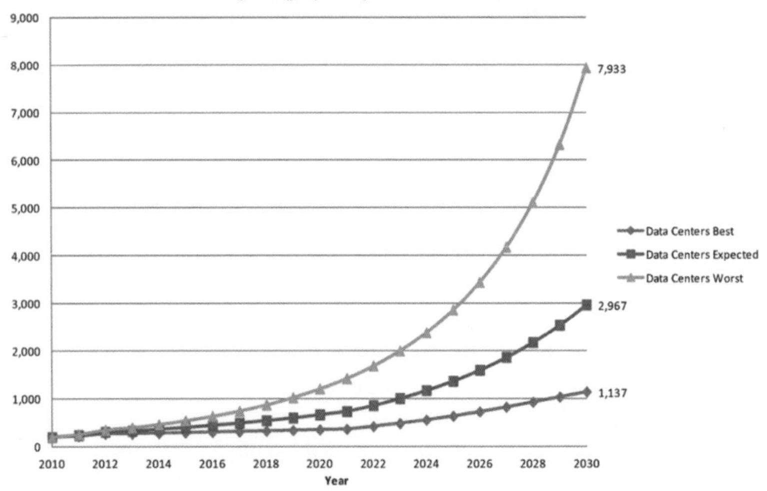

FIG 5.2: Even in the best-case scenario, data center energy is expected to rise massively over the next decade.

efits of simplification and miniaturization. If we're not going to host our projects in the back of a cupboard, then we need to embrace scale.

Going big

In recent years we've seen a trend called the *hyperscale shift*, led by big tech companies such as Amazon, Microsoft, and Google migrating these services out of the office or small data centers and into centralized, large-scale data centers. Hyperscale data centers embrace economies of scale to deliver lower costs, more advanced services, and higher levels of energy efficiency. On average, one server in a hyperscale data center is able to replace 3.75 servers in a conventional data center thanks to their highly optimized design (http://bkaprt.com/swd/01-01/).

The improvements in energy efficiency have been so profound that, despite significant growth in web traffic, the latest United States Data Center Energy Usage Report notes that "electricity consumption of data centers has been relatively flat in recent years." The report largely attributes this flatlining of energy consumption to the increasing use of "hyperscale data centers, where servers are often configured for maximum productivity and operated at higher utilization rates, resulting in fewer servers needed than would be required to provide the same services in traditional, smaller, data centers" (http://bkaprt.com/swd/05-02/, PDF).

The gains in efficiency have kept pace with our growing hunger for information, so we may well ask whether data center energy is even a significant issue to think about anymore. However, energy consumption is likely to begin increasing again as our industry finishes picking off most of the low hanging fruit to improve efficiency. Many data centers are now approaching the theoretical limit of power usage effectiveness (PUE), the standard measure of data center energy efficiency. As we approach this limit, it's likely that efficiency gains will plateau and global energy demand from data centers will again start to rise in line with growing data consumption.

The solution is twofold: we need to use the most efficient data centers we can find, but we also need to take responsibility for the applications we host, keeping energy requirements low to minimize their demand on servers.

Going small

David Cawsey's Raspberry Pi "data center" is at the far opposite end of the spectrum from modern hyperscale data centers, but it embraces the same principles of extreme efficiency. Following David's example, we can not only optimize our code to minimize the need for server resources, but we can also choose the smallest hosting service available to meet our needs, even if it is inside a gigantic data center. Perhaps we need more than a Raspberry Pi, but it's also likely we don't need the most powerful server.

If we can use a smaller server, then we can save energy *and* save money on hosting. We might feel a temptation to err on the side of caution and get a big server just to be sure it can handle our project's requirements. But if we've worked hard to optimize the efficiency of our website through the design and development process, the server requirements in terms of both storage and processing will be a fraction of other similar websites. The only way to find the optimal server size is to start small and test. Your hosting provider will be only too happy to help you scale up if you need to, whereas they aren't always so enthusiastic to help you scale down.

If you're worried about the risk of slow performance or downtime caused by your server being too small, try doing a soft launch first to test performance and gain confidence.

Shared hosting

The logical next step in shrinking the size of your servers is to not even have a whole server to yourself, but to share it with others. Shared hosting is a common offering from most hosting providers.

But is it always more efficient to have lots of customers sharing a server instead of dedicating a server to each application? As the Positive Internet Company cofounder Nick Mailer told me, it depends on what you need:

> *If you have one physical server's worth of work going on, then "virtualizing" it will actually just make things marginally less efficient. Where virtualization does become efficient is where want to carve up the hardware to do as much work as possible all the time: so rather than give someone a dedicated bit of hardware which spends much of the time sitting idle and heating up the room, you'd carve it up into virtualized environments so that when one VM was busy, another might be fallow, and so on. Thus, you "squeeze" as much potential out of the physical hardware as you can so that, hopefully, none is lying idle and just wasting power twiddling its thumbs.*

The key is to ensure that servers are well utilized at all times. In a presentation to Green Tech South West, Asim Hussain, green cloud advocacy lead at Microsoft, explained that "the more you do use hardware, the more efficient it becomes": since the server uses energy even when you're not using it, you get more usefulness for every gram of CO_2 produced over the server's life (http://bkaprt.com/swd/05-03/).

That said, we also need to make sure we don't try to "squeeze" too much out of a server. Tim Nash, a platform lead at hosting company 34SP, told me that overburdening a server with too many applications in a shared environment is also inefficient. Like Goldilocks's porridge, shared hosting has a sweet spot where we load the server not too much, not too little, but just right. Nash said that servers have an optimal load at which they run most efficiently:

> *A server running overprovisioned will end up in locking processes, so its high CPU and memory usage will become constant, whereas if the load was balanced across multiple servers, that locking wouldn't occur, memory gets released quicker, and the load is overall much smaller.*

What's more, overloaded servers generate a disproportionate amount of heat. This is a waste of the servers' energy, and that extra heat also has to be removed, demanding additional power load to the data center's cooling systems.

Of course, we should also consider the environmental impact of creating the physical hardware our applications run on. The same principle applies that underutilized servers are a waste of physical resources, but overutilized servers are also wasteful because the excessive strain on the hardware increases the odds of a hardware failure—thus shortening the life of the machine, increasing carbon emissions from the production of new servers, and increasing electronic waste.

So whether you should use shared or dedicated servers is not a simple question. If we have minimal server requirements and no specific technical need to have our own dedicated server, then a shared solution is likely going to be more efficient, but only if our hosting company is distributing their customers applications across servers to balance the load effectively. If we have specific requirements indicating we need more control over the server, then we might need a dedicated server—but that's unlikely to be for environmental reasons.

Content delivery networks

Content delivery networks (CDNs) are typically used to improve load times, but they also provide a useful function from an efficiency point of view. A significant proportion of the energy used by the average website is used in transmitting data through the telecom's networks from host to end user, wherever they might be in the world. CDNs improve on this by moving assets such as images, videos, and CSS files closer to the end user.

The closer you move the largest files towards your user base, the fewer *megabyte miles* the data needs to travel. A CDN might not benefit you much if 99 percent of your users are in the Netherlands and your web host is in Amsterdam, but if you have a highly international user base, then it makes sense to have copies of your largest files distributed globally so they don't have to travel all the way from Amsterdam every time they're requested.

CDNs are a great technology to help make the web more efficient, but we should remember that although they don't do the same data processing functions as standard hosting services, CDNs are themselves web hosts that store and serve a huge amount of data. You therefore should try to choose your CDN provider as carefully as you choose your main hosting provider and ensure they have a strong commitment to sustainability.

Finding a green CDN can be tricky, but like anything, it starts with asking the question. Every CDN provider has a sales team who will be only too happy to extol the virtues of their offering, and won't hesitate to tell you if they have a green energy commitment. Cloudflare was the first CDN provider to make any sort of renewable energy commitment, and in 2019 announced it would purchase renewable energy credits (RECs) to "match 100% of the power used in all those data centers and offices around the world" (http://bkaprt.com/swd/05-04/):

> *When combined with our ability to dramatically reduce the amount of data which has to flow through the Internet and the number of requests which have to reach our customer's origins we hope to not just be considered neutral, but to have*

a large-scale and long-term positive effect on the sustainability of the internet itself.

As we will see later, RECs aren't the most robust solution to renewable energy, but it's a step in the right direction. If CDN providers use renewable energy, then the service they offer in reducing server loads, reducing the distance that data has to travel, and blocking bots has a huge impact in reducing the carbon emissions of the web.

WHERE DOES THE ENERGY COME FROM?

We've examined how to make sure your hosting solution uses as little energy as possible, but where does that energy come from? According to a 2017 dataset from the International Energy Agency, only 23 percent of the world's electricity is currently generated from renewable sources, and 38 percent of electricity comes from burning (http://bkaprt.com/swd/05-05/).

What's more, one of the biggest clusters of data centers in the world, Data Center Alley, is co-located with some of the world's most polluting energy. Loudoun County in northern Virginia claims that 70 percent of the world's internet traffic passes through its borders (http://bkaprt.com/swd/05-06/). Despite being home to the data centers of some of the world's biggest tech companies, many of whom have made commitments to using green energy, Loudoun County generates a mere 5 percent of its electricity from renewable sources. According to Greenpeace, most of it comes from coal and fracked natural gas. The area's largest energy company, Dominion Energy, has resisted meaningful investment in renewable capacity and used continued growth in energy demand from data centers to justify significant investment in additional fossil fuel infrastructure, including $7 billion in the Atlantic Coast Pipeline (ACP) (http://bkaprt.com/swd/05-07/).

This should concern all of us who work in tech. We need not only public statements on the use of renewable energy, but meaningful action to green the energy infrastructure the web depends on, too. The internet is the largest coal-powered

FIG 5.3: Visit the Green Web Foundation and see if green hosting is available in your region (http://bkaprt.com/swd/05-08/).

machine ever created. This needs to change. If we want to stand any chance of tackling the climate crisis, we need the whole internet to be hosted in data centers powered by renewable energy.

That's the Green Web Foundation's mission. The foundation has created a comprehensive database of web hosts with a commitment to using green energy (**FIG 5.3**). Their data shows that 31 percent of websites are currently using "green" hosting providers. It's a great start and this number is rising, but we still have a long way to go.

How green is green?

Kris De Decker runs a publication called Low Tech Magazine and has created a solar-powered version of the website at solar.lowtechmagazine.com. He designed the website from the outset to use minimal energy, which means it can run on a mini computer with the processing power of a mobile phone. It needs just 1–2.5 watts of power, which is supplied by a small, off-grid, photovoltaic system on the balcony of De Decker's apartment in Barcelona.

LOW←TECH MAGAZINE

This is a solar-powered website, which means it sometimes goes offline

About | Low-tech Solutions | High-tech Problems | Obsolete Technology | Offline Reading | Archive | Donate |

Low-tech Solutions

Translations: es fr nl

How to Build a Low-tech Website?

Our new blog is designed to radically reduce the energy use associated with accessing our content.

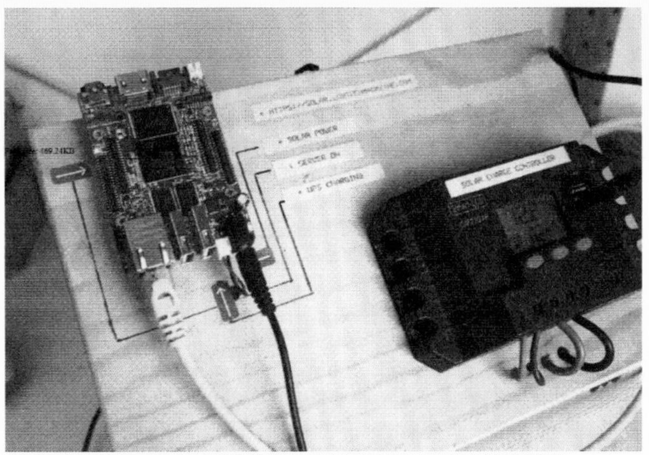

First prototype of the solar powered server that runs the new website. The solar charge controller (on the right) is powering the server (on the left) through a USB-cable

Low-tech Magazine: Kindle version.

Low-tech Magazine was born in 2007 and has seen minimal changes ever since. Because a website redesign was long overdue — and because we try to practice what we preach — we decided to build a low-tech, self-hosted, and solar-powered version of Low-tech Magazine. The new blog is designed to radically reduce the energy use associated with accessing our content.

FIG 5.4: Low Tech Magazine's solar version uses a yellow and blue background to indicate the website's available power. Dithered images help keep file sizes small.

Of course, the sun doesn't always shine, and that's a problem for web services we expect to be available 24/7. To solve this, Low Tech Magazine's solar panel is paired up with a lead-acid battery that stores excess energy when the sun is out, and continues to power the website during the night and on cloudy days.

The website even indicates the battery's state of charge via a background that changes from yellow (full battery) to blue (low battery) (**FIG 5.4**). Occasionally, if there isn't enough energy available from the solar panel or the battery, the website goes offline. That's not the end of the world for Low Tech Magazine, which also has a conventionally hosted version of its website and regards the solar version as an experiment and educational tool. However, it would be a problem for the majority of web services, and this is exactly why the idea of powering data centers with renewable energy is complicated.

De Decker points out that even this solution isn't truly zero carbon, because the solar and battery system themselves require a lot of energy to manufacture, negatively impacting the environment. He suggests that powering a single website from a dedicated solar system is not the most efficient solution, and that there are economies of scale in designing a system to power a larger number of websites. What's more, he points out that the energy of manufacturing the physical equipment highlights why using renewable energy is not enough; we must also try to use *less* energy (http://bkaprt.com/swd/05-09/).

A seemingly simple question of "how green is green?" is not so simple after all. On the surface, green hosting means that the server is directly connected to renewable power generators like solar panels, wind turbines, or hydro turbines in a similar manner to Low Tech Magazine's solar website. This is technically possible, but for commercial data centers, it's highly unusual.

Sure, there are some data centers that have solar panels on the roof or their own wind turbine outside, but they all have a connection to a larger energy grid from which they pull a significant portion of their electricity. Electrical grids are critical in distributing and balancing a region's energy needs, but when it comes to the supply of renewable energy, they make things a bit blurry. That's because if you pull energy from a shared electrical grid, you never really know where the electrons you're using came from (**FIG 5.5**).

Imagine electricity as being like tap water. Your local water company might have several sources of water including a natural mineral spring, a borehole, a rain-filled reservoir, and (hold your breath...) the treated water from your local sewage plant. Let's say they offered to sell you only 100 percent natural spring water in your home. You might be quick to sign up and even happy to pay a small premium, safe in the knowledge that you

FIG 5.5: To get from the middle of nowhere to the data center, renewable energy sources have to share the same energy grid as fossil fuel powered sources. (Photo by Tyler Casey on Unsplash)

can now quench your thirst with only the best quality water. However, the water coming out of your tap would not have changed. The only thing that would've changed is that they would have allocated your usage and payments to the production of the natural spring water in their accounts. That's it. Nothing actually changed and the water in your tap would be exactly the same. If your local water company did this, I think it's safe to say that you'd be outraged.

Well, that's exactly how electricity supplies work (http://bkaprt.com/swd/05-10/). Sure, you might not be drinking the emissions of a coal plant, but the impacts of burning fossil fuels are all too real. When you pay for 100 percent renewable energy, you expect 100 percent renewable energy. That bait-and-switch may make you think that renewable energy tariffs and green hosting are a con, and you would be partially right—but we mustn't throw the baby out with that slightly dubious bath water.

The truth is that in practice, this is the only way electricity grids can operate. And purchasing renewable energy—either as an individual, a business, a government or a hosting provider—

does have value. At the very least, it sends a clear signal to the energy market to show that there's growing demand for renewable sources of energy over fossil fuels (http://bkaprt.com/swd/05-11/). In the best cases, the money a customer spends on electricity (e.g. the data center) goes to the owners of the renewable energy supplies, helping them to out-compete other power companies and reinvest profits in building more renewables (http://bkaprt.com/swd/05-12/). Now that sounds more like it!

Knowing exactly what it means when a hosting company says it uses green energy is hard to decipher, because some energy contracts are more meaningful than others. The best way to find out what a web host's green energy commitment really means is to ask them. Generally they use some combination of the following types of renewable energy contracts:

- **Owning renewables:** They directly produce some or all of their own renewable energy onsite, or at least on the same energy grid. This is the most robust option, as it means they have taken responsibility for *generating* the electrons needed to power the data center.
- **Funding new renewables:** They sign *power purchase agreements* with energy companies that are designed to fund the construction of new renewable energy supplies in exchange for access to use that energy once it's available. In practice, this is about as robust as the first option, even if they don't own the wind turbines and solar panels themselves.
- **Buying renewable energy:** They purchase energy supplies from renewable energy generators that are on the same energy grid. Although they haven't helped create new renewable energy supplies, the renewable energy is being generated on the same grid the data center is drawing power from. Really, this should be the minimum standard of what can be claimed as "using renewable energy."
- **Buying credits:** They purchase *renewable energy credits* (RECs) from renewable energy generators on *other* grids. This basically involves finding renewable energy providers in other regions or countries, often poorer countries, and paying them some money to say they generated it for

you. This can help make renewable energy more profitable in those other countries and stimulate those markets, but unless they are actually on the same grid, those electrons will never reach your data center.
- **Carbon offsetting:** They purchase carbon offsets equivalent to the emissions produced by the nonrenewable power that fuels the data center. In many cases, carbon offsets simply pay someone else to reduce their emissions so that you don't have to. It doesn't directly address the issue of data centers being powered by fossil fuels, even if it can have some other benefits.

Most of the big tech companies are using a combination of these methods to move themselves towards what they view as 100 percent renewable energy (http://bkaprt.com/swd/05-13/):

- Google claims to have achieved 100 percent renewable energy in 2017 and has been a pioneer of power purchase agreements to help increase the amount of renewable capacity available on the grids they use. However, in practice only about 40 percent of their energy is from renewables directly on the same grid; in parts of the world where there is insufficient renewable capacity on the local grid, they still rely on purchasing RECs.
- Microsoft also claims to have achieved 100 percent renewable energy, with 60 percent coming from supplies on the same grid and the remaining 40 percent coming from RECs.
- Amazon made a commitment to transition to 100 percent renewable energy back in 2014, but exact details are vague. Greenpeace has accused them of abandoning this commitment, as they expanded their data center capacity in Virginia by 59 percent without adding any additional renewable capacity.

It's a step in the right direction, and any progress is progress, but we still have a long way to go before the big tech companies' services are *truly* powered by 100 percent renewable energy.

When does the sun shine?

The timing of when energy is generated needs to be matched with when energy is consumed. Unfortunately, the sun doesn't always shine and the wind doesn't always blow. It is easier to meet consumption with fossil fuel-fired turbines than it is with solar or wind energy.

Google has openly acknowledged this discrepancy and started monitoring how well a data center is matched with carbon-free energy on an hour-by-hour basis. Their ambition is to ensure that the local grid can supply enough renewable energy to their data centers, not just when averaged over a year, but on an hour-by-hour basis (http://bkaprt.com/swd/05-14/). In a discussion paper, they highlighted their data center in Hamima, Finland, as a case study of how this can be achieved. The Hamima data center is already achieving 97 percent renewable energy supply from the local grid when mapped hour by hour. They achieved this by securing power purchase agreements for more wind power than is needed by the data center, reducing the chances of there ever being too little renewable energy available on the local grid to supply the data center. As a consequence, Google often has a surplus of renewable energy that it can sell back to the grid in Finland.

This is a great start, but it's challenging to scale—partly because of the cost of building more renewable capacity than the data center will use, and also due to the fact that some parts of the world rely more heavily on solar, which doesn't generate any energy at night. The example of Low Tech Magazine using a battery to balance solar generation with website energy demand gives us a glimpse into the future of how this can be solved.

All data centers currently have backup generators running on kerosene or diesel. These generators fire up in the event of a power outage to keep their customers' web services online. They will need to be replaced with an alternative that doesn't depend on fossil fuels in the near future, and that's where batteries come in. Microsoft is already investing heavily in battery technology for their data centers and also running tests on hydrogen fuel cell generators, which could theoretically use hydrogen created with excess renewable energy (http://bkaprt.com/swd/05-13/).

To have data centers truly powered by 100 percent renewable energy, we'll need battery or fuel cell systems large enough to balance power generation and demand overnight, or even over several days. It's already happening. Switch data centers announced in mid-2020 that they have signed a deal with Tesla to provide 800 MWh of battery storage to pair with 550 MW of new solar energy capacity in Nevada (http://bkaprt.com/swd/05-15/). That's enough battery capacity to power three million miles of driving in Tesla's longest-range vehicles.

Coupling data centers with large-scale renewable energy generation and battery storage is a big shift and will require significant investment, but it could be highly profitable. Not only can it help data centers acquire low-cost renewable energy supplies, it would also enable data centers to capitalize on the fact that their own energy usage patterns are highly predictable. They will be able to purchase large volumes of cheap renewable energy when there is excess on the grid and then use it during times of shortage when grid energy is far more expensive.

Some commercial and domestic applications are already deploying battery storage systems using AI to predict energy requirements and energy prices (http://bkaprt.com/swd/05-16/). The clever part is that batteries allow not just storage of energy, but also the sale of electricity back to the grid, enabling electricity to be traded by AI in real time and profit from imbalances in supply and demand. It's surely only a matter of time before the tech industry capitalizes on this, not only to achieve 100 percent renewable energy supplies, but also to make a lot of money.

GOING FOR GREEN

Web hosting is a central part of the internet and therefore a central part of its environmental impact. Although the subtleties of green hosting are somewhat complex, the basic concepts of green energy and high energy efficiency are easy to grasp, and the process of switching hosts is generally fairly easy. Choosing a green host is therefore one of the lowest hanging fruits in creating more sustainable web services.

We should also remember that the principles of green hosting don't apply only to the hosts we choose for our main applications, but to all of the web services our applications depend on. If we're using a CDN, or hosting videos, or using a third-party payment provider, we should aim to select services with a strong commitment to sustainability in their own hosting infrastructure.

6 SELLING SUSTAINABLE WEB DESIGN

I WISH I COULD SAY digital sustainability sells itself. After all, who wouldn't want their web projects to be sustainable?

If we are designing and building things for ourselves, we can pursue sustainability as much as we like. However, many of us are working on digital projects for clients or for our employers, and sustainability is rarely in the brief.

This is for a couple of reasons. Awareness of web sustainability as a concept is frighteningly low. Even among environmentally minded techies, the fact that the internet and climate change are at all related is often a novel idea. The other reason is that even when people do know about it, they tend not to see it as a high priority. They might be happy with the idea of their web services being more sustainable, but low cost and aesthetics often take precedence.

How can we get our clients, employers, and colleagues on board with pursuing sustainable web design? Let's take a look.

BE A CHAMPION

The first step in selling sustainable web design to anyone is for you to step up and champion it. If sustainability sold itself, then we would already be living in a utopian circular economy powered entirely by renewable energy. But it doesn't, and so you need to be the person to put it on the agenda and say, "This is worth talking about."

As a sustainability champion, you might be surprised how much your enthusiasm can rub off on others. Things may not change overnight, but sustainability is a long game, and there is power in numbers. The more of us who vocally champion the cause, the faster it will sink into everyone's minds that sustainability is an essential topic.

If you want to sell it to clients, start by simply dropping it into conversations on a regular basis, lightly at first, and see how they respond. Likewise, if you're trying to get your boss or colleagues interested, then talking about it openly as something you care deeply about is the first step to seeding the concept in their minds.

Don't stop at only having conversations, though. Embrace whatever channels you have available to talk about sustainability in relation to web work, whether through conference talks, blog posts, articles, or social media (**FIG 6.1**). It all helps to plant the seeds.

SOLVE PEOPLE'S PROBLEMS

Motivating people to take real action is the hard part. If you're trying to inspire clients to embrace sustainability in your projects together, remember the basic principles that apply to selling *any* aspect of a web project. The client isn't spending their money out of the goodness of their heart or as a hobby project—they have real business goals they're trying to achieve. Even if they personally care about the environment, they won't see digital sustainability as relevant to their project unless you can show them how it aligns with their goals. This doesn't just apply to external clients, but also to internal teams working on

FIG 6.1: When I presented at WordCamp Europe 2017, it seemed nobody had heard of sustainable web design. (Video image from WordPress.tv.)

digital products, where the company management is effectively the client.

Ben Clifford, who runs eco-focused web agency Erjjio Studios, told me he has encountered this in his work:

> *Even for clients who are heavily interested in sustainability, it's still not always their key consideration, sadly—overall design, functionality, cost, convenience, and reliability are still the major priorities, and sometimes this is at the expense of sustainability.*

We've had a similar experience at Wholegrain Digital, with sustainability rarely (if ever) being at the top of the client's priority list. We've found that the key to success isn't to try selling "sustainable web design," but to sell the client what they really want. Focus on solving the client's specific problems first, while using sustainability as a tool to solve those problems. As sustainable web design has so many benefits, it's nearly always possible to find something high on the client's priority list—such as SEO, conversion rates, or accessibility—that can pave the way for pursuing more sustainable solutions.

Digital agency Mightybytes has been offering sustainable web design services since way back in 1998, and CEO Tim Frick told me he's reached the same conclusion:

> *As time passed, we evolved our sales messaging. While the green angle didn't seem to resonate with customers, the performance angle did, especially when they were reminded that most users will leave a slow website. Equating website performance with the bottom line turned out to be a good driver for adopting these practices. Reducing website greenhouse gas emissions is a priority for us as an agency, so we simply baked sustainable web design practices into the process of building any and all client websites.*

The trick is to find out what the customer truly cares about, and use that as a lever to deliver more sustainable solutions. Here are some angles to help you explore sustainable web design with your clients:

- **User experience:** Many website owners are aware of the importance of good UX in delivering high conversion rates, high customer satisfaction, and positive brand perception. By prioritizing streamlined, intuitive user journeys, fast load times, and offline functionality, we can create great experiences for our users no matter where they are. This leads to better commercial outcomes for the website owner *and* reduces carbon emissions in the process.
- **SEO:** Most website owners care about their search engine rankings, and sustainable web design can help. Google uses load speed as a ranking factor in its search listings, with some priority going to faster sites. The pursuit of efficiency in the web design and development process ensures good web performance and therefore helps improve search rankings.
- **Accessibility:** Accessibility is a key issue every organization should take seriously, but especially those serving marginalized groups. Public bodies, NGOs, and organizations operating in developing countries are particularly likely to attend to this. If their target audience cannot access the website—whether due to poor connectivity, slow devices,

or the high cost of data—then it doesn't matter how good the website is in other regards. Using sustainability as a lens in our projects can help deliver services that are more accessible to a wider audience.

- **Security:** For organizations that consider security a high priority, going the extra mile and embracing solutions such as firewalls and static web technology can add an extra layer of protection while also delivering reduced carbon emissions.
- **Uptime:** It sounds obvious, but websites can only deliver their purpose when they're online. Uptime is therefore important for every website, but for some, it's absolutely critical. If the client sees their website as a reflection of their brand, then they're going to want to ensure it's always online and making a good impression on the world. If their website has an ecommerce element, then downtime can literally cost money in lost sales. And for public information sites, especially those serving vulnerable people, always being available is essential. Prioritizing resilience through approaches such as CDNs, static web technology, and offline functionality can directly support the interests of the client.
- **Hosting costs:** For high-traffic websites, web hosting can become a major ongoing cost. As traffic increases, the infrastructure required to handle the heavy server load and bandwidth usage can become both a technical and a financial burden on the project. Many of the approaches of sustainable web design help by minimizing server load and the amount of data transferred to each user.

As for persuading the client to use a green hosting supplier, it's unlikely to directly solve their project goals. However, in most cases, switching to another host is a fairly minor job, and there is no cost premium for hosting with a green provider, so there isn't a downside. On the upside, the client would gain the reputational benefit of being able to state that their website runs on renewable powered servers and have their website show positively when measured through tools like Ecograder, Website Carbon Calculator, and The Green Web Foundation database.

BUILD A BETTER TEAM

In a 2019 report, independent think tank Doteveryone found that significant numbers of highly skilled people in the tech industry are leaving jobs they feel could have negative consequences for people and society, at considerable expense to their employers. The report found that 63 percent of tech workers said they would like more opportunity to talk about ethical issues in their projects, and 78 percent would like more practical resources to help them do so (http://bkaprt.com/swd/06-01/, PDF).

One truth is common to all organizations: people are their greatest asset. Developing an organizational culture in which issues such as climate change are openly discussed and teams are empowered to make positive choices requires investment—but it's an investment that can easily pay for itself in staff retention. If you're trying to sell web sustainability to your boss, this is probably one of the strongest arguments you can make.

Organizations should also think about indirect benefits of building such a culture, such as the reduced cost of recruitment and the ability to attract more talent. Organizations taking a forward-thinking approach to web sustainability may find it easier to attract and retain talent in digital teams, increasing the caliber of staff in their organization and reducing the cost and disruption of staff turnover.

At this time in history when climate change is the existential issue facing our generation, embedding sustainable practices at the core of our work adds real meaning to what we do, whatever that happens to be. It can ignite a spark within people that spurs them on to show up each day and give their best. And when people give their best, the organizations they work for thrive.

My colleague Rachael Blair summed it up nicely: "People now don't just want a 'job,' but to be part of something bigger, to do work that they really believe in, and to make a positive difference in the world" (http://bkaprt.com/swd/06-02/).

GET ON THE GOOD SIDE OF GOVERNMENT

Whether we're trying to sell sustainable web design to our clients or to our colleagues, it's worth considering that the attitudes and actions of governments may provide a real incentive worth planning ahead for.

Procurement

As I mentioned in Chapter 1, governments are the single largest customers for products and services in any country, and they have the potential to influence markets through their procurement decisions. Even if it hasn't happened yet, as climate change rises in priority on the global political agenda, it becomes a question of *when*, not *if*, they will introduce sustainability as criteria in their procurement of digital services.

In 2020, the European Commission's flagship Next Generation Internet (NGI) initiative published a report on how Europe can create greener and more digitally connected socioeconomic policy, stating:

> *While consumer behavior is important, public bodies such as national and local governments spend billions of euros on internet technology each year. These bodies procure digital technologies at such enormous scales that even small changes in strategy and policy lifecycle could drastically reduce environmental impact. (http://bkaprt.com/swd/06-03/, PDF)*

In any country, the government is one of the biggest purchasers of IT services, putting it in a position to use its financial power, rather than just political power, to influence industry practices. We're talking a substantial amount of funding; in 2020, the United States federal government budget allotted *$87 billion* toward information technology (http://bkaprt.com/swd/06-04/, PDF). Imagine if every single contract had a requirement for organizations to submit their carbon footprint data and specified carbon accounting for digital projects. We would very quickly see sustainability take high priority on the tech industry's agenda.

When governments do start including sustainability as procurement criteria for digital services, organizations that have already embraced sustainability in their work will have a significant advantage in winning government contracts. If you work on projects in or for the public sector, then this is something worth taking seriously. Being proactive and getting ahead of the competition now will put you in a strong position to win government contracts down the line.

Regulation

If government procurement is the carrot, then regulations are the stick. Web sustainability might not currently be a part of specific government regulations in the way web accessibility is in some countries, but there are good reasons to believe it will happen. With emissions from internet services rising rapidly, without some form of environmental regulation to tackle it, governments will struggle to meet their obligations under the Paris Agreement. The question, really, is what form these regulations will take.

There are many possibilities: directly enforcing sustainability standards in digital projects, labeling digital products for energy efficiency and carbon footprint (as is already the case for vehicles and electrical appliances in many countries), establishing limits on the amount and type of energy consumed by data centers and telecoms networks, and more.

Even if environmental regulations specific to the digital sector never materialize, we can be fairly sure that general regulations on carbon emissions will become more stringent and cover all sectors, directly or indirectly. This could be in the form of hard limits, or some form of carbon tax.

Just as with government procurement, when this happens, the organizations that got ahead of the game will have an inherent competitive advantage. Tommy Ricketts, CEO of decarbonization company BeZero, told me that he makes the case to his clients that they only have two choices: take action now to innovate your own solutions to inevitable regulation, or wait until the government forces you to take action—at which point it will be a sudden, expensive, and disruptive transition, with the government calling the shots and little in the way of positive outcomes for you commercially.

Which of those sounds more appealing? This could be a compelling argument to take to your company's management, or even to your clients. Getting ahead of the game on government regulation is the wise move.

A UNIQUE SELLING POINT?

Whether you work for a company that makes digital products, or one offering web design and development services to other organizations, there's a good chance you operate in a competitive marketplace and are always looking for a way to differentiate your offering. This could be a compelling argument for persuading your boss to take web sustainability seriously. Even if they don't care about the issue directly, they might be excited by the possibility of a competitive edge.

However, I'm cautious about recommending this as an approach to selling sustainable web design within your organization for two reasons.

Firstly, as I mentioned in Chapter 1, greenwashing is a significant threat to climate solutions. When organizations make "green" claims to make themselves look good but don't truly care about the issues, it's worse than doing nothing. It perpetuates a false sense of security in the public that progress is being made when often it is not. Furthermore, misleading information confuses both employees and customers, and leads to a sense of disillusionment about the issues that really matter. Sustainable web design should only be used as a unique selling point if the people within your organization truly care about the issues, are committed to tackling them with real solutions, and are prepared to be honest about the success or failure of those initiatives.

Secondly, while it's positive and exciting in many ways that people are now taking an interest in organizations committed to sustainability, it also worries me. Sustainability should not be a niche or a novelty. We need to be creating a world in which sustainability is the default, not the exception. Low-carbon web design shouldn't be a unique selling point—it should be the industry standard.

In the short term, sustainable design will serve as a differentiator for organizations that embrace it wholeheartedly. But we should work towards a future where sustainable practices are no longer so rare they make us stand out from the crowd.

WE HAVE NOTHING TO LOSE

In a popular cartoon drawn by Joel Pett for USA Today (http://bkaprt.com/swd/06-05/), a presenter at a climate summit stands before a screen that lists the benefits of pro-environmental action: "Energy independence, clean water, air, healthy children, etc." A man in the audience stands up to ask, "What if it's a big hoax and we create a better world for nothing?"

What if this book is a big hoax, and the internet doesn't contribute to climate change at all? You'll have spent all this time reading about sustainable web design principles that help us create a faster, more accessible, more enjoyable, easier to use, and more resilient internet. Would that be so bad?

THE INTERNET IN A CHANGING CLIMATE

CLIMATE CHANGE IS ALREADY HERE, and it's already impacting the reliability of the web. It's important for us to recognize that this is just the beginning. Because of a phenomenon called *climate lag*, emissions don't impact the planet's climate instantaneously. James Hansen, climate scientist and former director of NASA's Goddard Institute for Space Studies, puts typical climate lag at between twenty-five and fifty years (http://bkaprt.com/swd/07-01/). That means we are today experiencing the effects of emissions generated during the 1970s–1990s. Even if we stop emitting greenhouse gases today, we've guaranteed that climate change will get significantly worse over the next few decades because we've already emitted vast amounts of greenhouse gases over the past few decades. We are locked in.

We're currently designing for the web with the assumption that the internet will only ever be better than it is now, and for everyone. Yet much of the infrastructure we depend on for internet services was never designed with climate change in mind.

We therefore need to ensure that the internet is designed to function in a changing and less hospitable world. As we look ahead to an exciting future with AI, VR, and every imaginable object connected, we need to plan ahead and prioritize resilience *before* we need it.

WATER, WIND, AND HEAT

London Docklands, stretching along the River Thames in London, is the epicenter of internet data flowing through, in, and out of the UK. It's home to a number of large data centers and points of presence, where individual data centers connect to the wider internet. It also faces serious flood risk from sea level rise (**FIG 7.1**). Nick Mailer told me he looked at the Docklands before deciding instead to locate their data center on higher ground in Cambridgeshire:

> *The Docklands is on a floodplain, and it's only thanks to the Thames Barrier that it doesn't actually flood. But the Thames Barrier is not infallible, never more so than when sea levels rise. We noted that quite a few emergency generators were in basements of the London Dockland data centers, with grating for their vents. We did indeed imagine what would happen were the area to be flooded, and we were not reassured. In effect, the Docklands is the UK's internet "switchboard." If the London Docklands were to be damaged or disconnected, then the result for the UK's internet would be calamitous.*

Sea levels won't affect only data centers, but also the cables that connect us to the web. A study by the University of Oregon and the University of Wisconsin-Madison looked at internet infrastructure in the United States and found that, in the next fifteen years, 4,067 miles of fiber internet cables are likely to be permanently underwater, and 1,101 nodes (points of presence and colocation centers) will be surrounded by sea water (http://bkaprt.com/swd/07-03/, PDF). That's just in the United States. Of course it won't happen overnight, but in the long run it

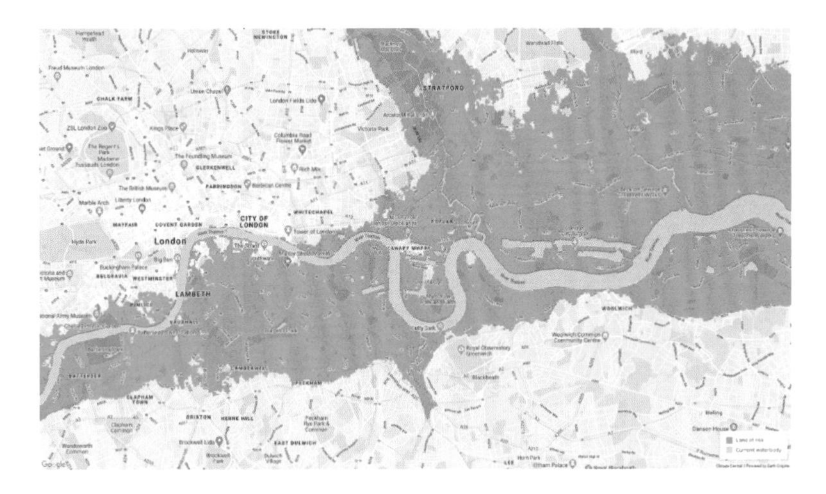

FIG 7.1: Projected flood levels in 2050 in a moderate scenario, showing London Docklands at the center. Map generated via Climate Central (http://bkaprt.com/swd/07-02/).

could disrupt the performance and reliability of the web we depend on.

The risks of coastal flooding from rising sea levels are exacerbated by storms that push the sea inland. These storms are growing in frequency and strength, and bring with them high winds that threaten other internet infrastructure, such as cell towers and power supplies to data centers.

And this is all before we even mention the basic fact that the world is getting warmer. One of the big costs of running data centers is keeping the machines cool. As global temperatures rise, the energy required to cool data centers will rise significantly, creating a feedback loop in which climate change increases the energy use and carbon emissions of the internet, which in turn accelerate climate change. It seems that one of our key strategies to keep the internet running smoothly in an increasingly hostile climate will be to burn more fuel. As Hurricane Florence approached the East Coast of the United States in 2018, Robert Fiordaliso, director of critical infrastructure at data center operator CenturyLink, described the backup power plans in place:

I have 50,000 gallons of fuel on site to refuel generators...In addition we have several 10,000-gallon tankers, or motherships, just outside the predicted storm strike zone, and those are serviced by smaller trucks containing 2,500 or 5,000 gallons that can be pulled to sites by trucks. (http://bkaprt.com/swd/07-04/)

That's a lot of fossil fuel ready to be burned in backup generators when the data center is hit by the worst effects of climate change.

COMMUNICATION IN CRISIS

As wildfires swept through Australia in late 2019 and early 2020, destroying an area of land twice the size of Belgium, many people in danger found they had limited or no access to mobile phone networks and data. As cell towers were destroyed or damaged by fire, access to information and communication channels was cut off precisely when and where people needed it most. The issue was compounded by the fact that intense fire releases plasma, which interferes with certain radio frequencies, degrading signal strength even when the towers are operational (http://bkaprt.com/swd/07-05/). Telco operators asked the Australian government to be added to a priority list for fuel during emergencies in order to run emergency generators, stating that power loss is the largest cause of communications blackouts in wildfire areas (**FIG 7.2**).

It wasn't just mobile towers that failed, though; the National Broadband Network (NBN) also struggled during the wildfires. Amanda Leck, director of community safety at Australia's National Council for Fire and Emergency Services, said they had been expressing concern about the NBN's ability to withstand a natural disaster for a couple of years. In her words, "We all knew that the NBN would crap out almost immediately, and it did" (http://bkaprt.com/swd/07-07/).

The COVID-19 pandemic in 2020 highlighted a new challenge, as millions of office workers began working from home. While this temporarily had a positive impact on the environment and air quality, it also put extra strain on the web, with

FIG 7.2: The Australian wildfires in 2020 impacted people on a scale that is hard to comprehend. Photo by Joshua Stevens/NASA (http://bkaprt.com/swd/07-06/).

peak internet traffic up by 30 percent in Italy, according to Cloudflare (http://bkaprt.com/swd/07-08/). Thankfully, the internet held up well overall, but many people experienced degraded performance. It's a glimpse into a future where we may need to travel a lot less and rely on internet services to a far greater extent.

As the impacts of climate change grow, large tech companies will have the financial resources to protect their infrastructure and commercial services, while smaller businesses will struggle to maintain resilient systems. In an article for the *New Republic*, Greenpeace IT specialist Gary Cook suggested that this economic disparity will also be apparent among web users: "Customers with the wherewithal to pay for more reliable services will still get [them], and there will be a wider divide between

CNN | 4/11/2020 | Listen

Main Stories

- Analysis: America can't beat the coronavirus crisis until we fix what really ails us
- More than 2,000 US coronavirus deaths reported in a day, likely a peak toll, expert says
- The 115-year-old Supreme Court opinion that could determine rights during a pandemic
- Colorado meat packing plant with thousands of employees closed after coronavirus outbreak
- A crisis mental-health hotline has seen an 891% spike in calls
- Exclusive: Navy commander says virus-struck aircraft carrier crew 'struggling' after captain's firing
- Trump keeps wanting to reopen the economy. Voters disagree.
- Trump administration shuttered pandemic monitoring program, then scrambled to extend it
- Trump spends Easter weekend pondering the 'biggest decision' of his presidency
- The Depression-era government gave artists jobs, we may need a similar program today
- President Trump is wrong in so many ways about hydroxychloroquine studies. Here are the facts
- 10 leaders who mattered most on coronavirus response this week
- Fact-checking the Trump campaign's deceptive new anti-Biden ad
- A grandmother sang 'Happy Birthday' to herself in a heartwarming video while quarantined due to the coronavirus
- Health care workers are wearing smiling photos of themselves to put coronavirus patients at ease
- These hospice workers find creative ways to bring light during a pandemic
- Must-watch videos of the week
- Sweden challenges Trump -- and scientific mainstream -- by refusing to lock down

FIG 7.3: CNN Lite makes the latest news accessible on even the slowest connections.

those who do and don't" (http://bkaprt.com/swd/07-09/). On a typical day, that might not make much difference, but in crisis situations, it will have a profoundly negative impact on small businesses and vulnerable citizens.

But web services can be designed to be more resilient to our changing climate. As Hurricane Irma approached the United States in 2017, CNN announced that they had launched a text-only version of their website to ensure that people affected by the storm could still access critical news with only a minimal data connection required (**FIG 7.3**). The homepage of the text-only site is 97.5 percent smaller than the main CNN website, making it not just low-carbon, but also far more accessible. It was extremely well received, as it ensured that many people had access to critical information even when the wired broadband and 3G/4G networks were down (http://bkaprt.com/swd/07-10/).

It's a great example of the type of solutions we need to be developing in the future, contrasting our rich-immersive digital experiences with simple, no-frills solutions for the services we depend on.

Low bandwidth, better experience

That said, creating a secondary version of a website to cater to suboptimal conditions is not ideal. Just as we've moved away from building separate mobile websites to building responsive sites that work on all devices, we should aim to follow the same approach when it comes to websites that can function on low bandwidth connections. If we embrace efficiency as a core requirement from the very outset of our projects, we can create rich web experiences that are *also* low bandwidth. The result isn't just greater resilience of the full web service we've created, but faster load times for everyone, even in perfect conditions.

The COVID-19 guide from Gov.UK provides key information to the general public about how to stay safe during the pandemic (**FIG 7.4**) (http://bkaprt.com/swd/07-11/). It needs to be accessible to the widest possible audience, no matter what device or connection they have. The full page is just 263 KB and achieves a score of 100 percent in Google PageSpeed. It's a good example of efficient design and development supporting the public during a crisis by making information easy to access.

We also need to eliminate single points of failure. The team behind Digital.gov has embraced JAMstack for a new version of their site, using the static site generator Hugo (**FIG 7.5**). By using static files on a CDN, they've improved load times for users, as well as ensuring that crucial content is accessible even if a data center goes offline. Decoupling the CMS from the front end also avoids the risk of overloading the server hosting the CMS during high-traffic crises. Yes, you can get some of these benefits without using a JAMstack solution, but there's an inherent resiliency with this approach that isn't found in more traditional website configurations.

Improved resilience has benefits beyond the duty-bound services of government and news websites—it's a key pillar of good customer service for all sorts of organizations serving customers online. Take none other than Starbucks, for example. When creating a browser-based ordering system, Starbucks wanted to ensure that customers' orders wouldn't be disrupted by unreliable mobile connections. Their digital agency, Formi-

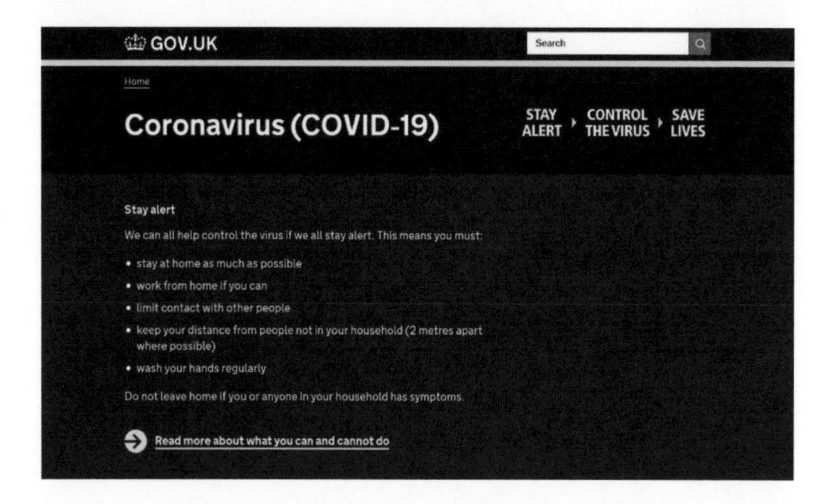

FIG 7.4: Efficient and accessible web design supporting the public in a crisis.

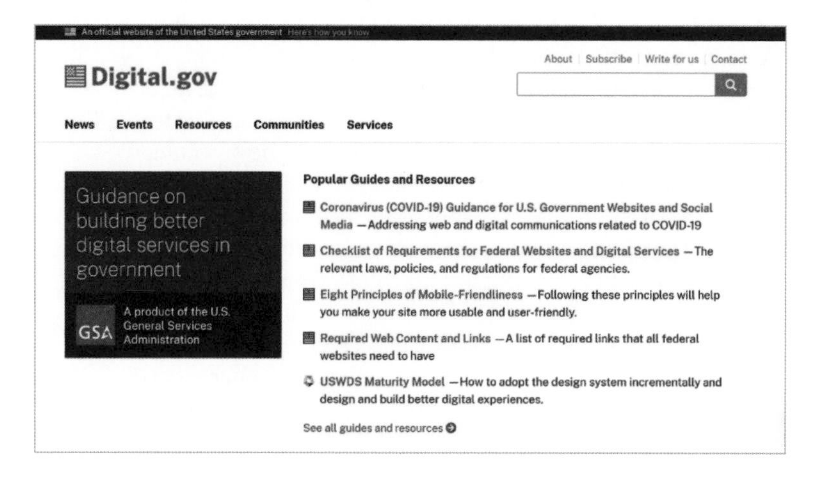

FIG 7.5: Digital.gov uses the Hugo static site generator (http://bkaprt.com/swd/07-12/).

dable, used Progressive Web App technology to enable as much of the ordering process as possible to function offline:

> *In order to create the offline functionality for the PWA, complex caching had to be set up to download the information for each menu item, store information on customers' previous orders, and store static pages from the website.* (*http://bkaprt.com/swd/07-13/*)

Ordering a coffee may seem like an overly simple use case, but this type of approach is exactly what we'll need to create a resilient web across any number of services.

Beyond the browser

The previous examples assume that the user has some access to the internet via a data connection and web browser. But how would we provide information to users who can't access websites at all?

WeFarm is an SMS-based crowdsourcing service to help farmers in developing countries—who rarely have internet access and tend to live in isolated areas—find the information they need, source supplies, and determine pricing (http://bkaprt.com/swd/07-14/). Farmers send questions to WeFarm via SMS; using machine learning, the WeFarm system interprets the questions and forwards them to farmers with relevant experience, who then send answer back via SMS. The system allows farmers to access information quickly, without an internet connection, and for only the cost of a standard SMS.

We must challenge our own assumptions and think deeply about the true problems we are trying to solve. Is our job to *design a website*, or is it to provide users access to information and services? By focusing on the true problems to be solved, we might just find some creative solutions.

Orbiting possibilities

If the earth's climate poses such a great threat to infrastructure, we might also ask whether we could eliminate the climate itself from the equation somehow. One interesting idea is the creation of a high-speed, low-latency satellite internet—a growing possibility as tech companies such as SpaceX enter a new space race. Although climate change isn't the motivating factor for these new networks, they may provide a far more resilient solution to transferring data around the globe without being impacted by wind, floods, wildfires, and rising temperatures. Plus, they would offer far greater coverage in rural parts of the world where it's simply too expensive to build high-speed cable or mobile infrastructure.

You might be wondering how ecofriendly it is to put satellites into space. The SpaceX program plans to launch forty-two thousand satellites into the Earth's orbit. That sounds like a lot of rocket fuel, but the CO_2 released by launching these satellites is roughly equivalent to that of five full passenger planes journeying from London to Sydney (http://bkaprt.com/swd/07-15/).

That's a fraction of what it would take to build physical infrastructure on the ground covering the entire globe. Plus, the satellites themselves are solar-powered, minimizing the energy and emissions required for transferring data twenty-four hours a day once they're in operation. The downside is that, by definition, these networks will be owned and controlled by a small number of powerful companies, and that brings about its own challenges.

For web designers, a satellite network could help us deliver web services to a much wider audience currently excluded from our digital world. And by embracing resiliency to maintain steady communication amid fluctuating climate circumstances, we can maximize the benefits to these new web users. This is how we can create a web that adapts to what users need, rather than demanding they adapt to limited networks and service providers.

A RESILIENT FUTURE

Ensuring fast, reliable, and open access to the internet for the world's citizens is going to be a growing challenge as the large-scale impacts of climate change begin to take effect. The good news is that many of the approaches we can use to create a more climate-friendly web are the same approaches that will help us create a more resilient web. When we pull together approaches such as static web technology, content delivery networks, offline functionality, and communication technologies like SMS, we can create web services that stand up to almost *anything*.

If we approach it positively, this challenge will lead us to more creative solutions for a web that is better for everyone.

CONCLUSION

WE'RE AT A CRITICAL TIME in history where we must choose what future we want. We can continue with business as usual, which is easy in the short term but locks us into a dystopian future—or we can take action, and rapidly transition to a cleaner, fairer, and more sustainable society.

The internet will be an important part of our future, but it, on its own, will not decide which version of the future that will be. That's up to us: an increasingly bloated web driven by ever-increasing consumption, or a hyper-efficient, socially conscious digital sector powered entirely by renewable energy.

A sustainable web is possible. A web that isn't just compatible with a zero-carbon future, but also supports our transition to that future. A web that is accessible to all, even in times of crisis, and is faster, more enjoyable to use, and potentially more profitable.

For those of us who work in digital, creating a sustainable internet is *our* job. We cannot expect the public to go on a data diet or wait for governments to implement regulatory solutions. It's our responsibility, as the people who build and maintain the hardware and software of the internet, to make sure our work creates the future we want and need.

There is no downside to a sustainable web, and creating it isn't fundamentally difficult. In fact, it's one of the most tangible and achievable steps in the zero-carbon revolution we're embarking on. For a sustainable web to become a reality only requires us to be aware of the issues and have the guts to challenge the status quo in making it a priority.

We are rapidly running out of time, but we can succeed if we act now. To paraphrase Doc Brown in *Back to the Future*, our future is whatever we make it—so let's make it a good one.

ACKNOWLEDGMENTS

WRITING A BOOK ON SUSTAINABLE design has been an ambition of mine for a long time. I've had many false starts and the fact that I finally wrote it is thanks in part to many people. So, here goes the embarrassing Oscar's speech!

This book is in many ways not my work, but a dissemination of the amazing work that my wonderful team at Wholegrain Digital have done together with our clients over the past few years. Even though my name is on the cover, this book combines of all of our shared efforts to explore, create, and promote a greener web.

I must say a special thanks to Rachael Blair, who has been gently encouraging me to write a book for a long time, helping me improve as a writer, and without whom I might never have found the confidence to make this book happen. Likewise, my friend Alex Denning of Ellipsis Marketing, who has been a huge help over the past couple of years in helping me to find my voice as a writer. And thanks to my friend Stephie, who unwittingly lit the blue touch paper and spurred me to finally write this book by asking me what I *really* want to do.

Having taken that plunge, Katel LeDû and Lisa Maria Marquis were generous enough to believe in my vision and give me this opportunity to write for A Book Apart to bring this topic to a wider audience. From that point forward, the whole team at ABA have worked incredibly hard, been a great support, and kept me laughing even when it got hard.

And then there are all the wonderful and forward-thinking people in the web and business communities that I have enjoyed being a part of, including those in the Sustainable UX and ClimateAction.Tech communities, not to mention the amazing B Corp community, my friends in the Happy Porch agency group, and the coauthors and signatories of the Sustainable Web Manifesto, an initiative that has provided a foundation for this book in many ways. Particular thanks to Tim Frick, Chris Adams, Mike Gifford, Jack Lenox, Marketa Benisek, Nick

Mailer, Neil Clark, and Hannah Smith for being much-needed positive voices in our industry and encouraging me on my own journey. All have taught me so much and inspired me to keep pushing for a better world and a better web.

I spent a lot of time researching this book, and I'm really grateful to all the people who spent the time talking with me, advising me, and sharing information and case studies to bring this book to life.

Finally, this book wouldn't be more than a glint in my eye if it wasn't for the support of my wonderful wife Vineeta, who fueled this book with enthusiasm, love, and an endless supply of delicious food!

RESOURCES

TO INCLUDE EVERY USEFUL resource on this topic would fill another book. Instead, I've tried to highlight those that are most valuable or have had the biggest influence on me.

Climate change books

- *This Changes Everything* by Naomi Klein. I have cared about the environment for a long time, but this book really did change everything for me, and perhaps it will for you too.
- *The Uninhabitable Earth* by David Wallace-Wells. A beautifully written but deeply dark account of the business-as-usual future we are creating. Not for the fainthearted.
- *The Future We Choose: Surviving the Climate Crisis* by Christiana Figueres and Tom Rivett-Carnac. Written by two leading figures of the Paris Agreement, this book will give you hope.
- *No One is Too Small to Make a Difference* by Greta Thunberg. This tiny book contains Greta's speeches and belongs next to the bed for small doses of inspiration.

Sustainable design and business books

- *Design for the Real World* by Victor Papanek. This is one of the first books to promote the idea of ethics and the environment in design. It may be old, but it's full of wisdom and gives us a glimpse back into the world of design before the internet.
- *The Green Imperative: Ecology and Ethics in Design and Architecture* by Victor Papanek. Another classic, focusing on the relationship between design and the natural environment.
- *Let My People Go Surfing* by Yvon Chouinard. The founder and owner of Patagonia sets out his incredible vision and shares his experiences in trying to create a responsible business.
- *Design for Sustainability* by Tim Frick. Another great book on the environmental aspects of digital design.
- *World Wide Waste* by Gerry McGovern. An emotive deep dive into the oceans of waste in the digital sector.

Digital Sustainability Communities

- Sustainable UX. A Slack community full of wonderful people pursuing greener digital design. They also hold an annual online conference (http://bkaprt.com/swd/08-01/).
- ClimateAction.Tech. A Slack community for sharing ideas, information, and experiences in all aspects of tackling climate change as a digital professional. They also organize meetups around the world (http://bkaprt.com/swd/08-02/).

Email newsletters

- Curiously Green. A monthly newsletter produced by my team at Wholegrain Digital, covering news, ideas, and content for anyone curious about web sustainability. If you're reading this book, I guess that's you (http://bkaprt.com/swd/08-03/)!
- Greening Digital. A regular email newsletter produced by Chris Adams, sharing his learnings in web sustainability (http://bkaprt.com/swd/08-04/).
- HEATED. A newsletter from climate journalist Emily Atkin showcasing great investigative reporting on climate and accountability, with excellent explainers for knotty legislative issues and murky corporate practice (http://bkaprt.com/swd/08-05/).

Sustainable web design tools and frameworks

- The Sustainable Web Manifesto. Outlines six core principles to guide you in pursuing sustainability in your work. Read and sign (http://bkaprt.com/swd/08-06/).
- Website Carbon. A calculator that helps you understand the carbon impact of a web page. You can embed their badge in the footer of your website (http://bkaprt.com/swd/08-07/).
- Ecograder. A holistic tool to help identify aspects of your website that may impact its sustainability (http://bkaprt.com/swd/08-08/).

- PerformanceBudget.io. A handy tool for calculating a performance budget, which can also be used as the basis for a carbon budget (http://bkaprt.com/swd/08-09/).
- The Green Web Foundation. A database and one of the best places to find a green hosting provider. The Chrome browser extension is educational too (http://bkaprt.com/swd/05-08/).
- Granola. The WordPress framework designed by my team at Wholegrain Digital for optimal efficiency (http://bkaprt.com/swd/08-10/).
- Image optimization. There are numerous tools for optimizing images including ImageOptim (http://bkaprt.com/swd/08-11/), ShortPixel (http://bkaprt.com/swd/08-12/) and TinyPNG (http://bkaprt.com/swd/08-13/). ImageAlpha is great for hand-optimizing PNG files (http://bkaprt.com/swd/08-14/), and WebP Express is an excellent WordPress plugin for automatically converting images to WEBP format (http://bkaprt.com/swd/08-15/).
- Doteveryone's Consequence Scanning toolkit. Download it for free to help you run your own workshops to identify any unintended consequences of your projects (http://bkaprt.com/swd/08-16/).
- The Carbon Footprint calculator. A very handy tool for calculating emissions from your business operations and lifestyle (http://bkaprt.com/swd/08-17/).
- The B Impact Assessment. The backbone of the B Corp Certification. You can use the assessment tool online for free to learn about how you can operate your business even more responsibly (http://bkaprt.com/swd/08-18/).

Publications

- "Global Warming of 1.5°C." A special report from the Intergovernmental Panel on Climate Change on the state of the world's climate (http://bkaprt.com/swd/08-19/).
- "How to stop data centers from gobbling up the world's electricity" by Nicola Jones. A good overview of the energy impacts and possible solutions to data center energy consumption (http://bkaprt.com/swd/08-20/).

- "On Global Electricity Usage of Communication Technology: Trends to 2030" by Anders Andrae and Tomas Edler. One of the most comprehensive and credible studies on the energy consumption of the web, including a downloadable dataset (http://bkaprt.com/swd/08-21/).

You can also find regular articles on the sustainability challenges and solutions in both business and digital projects on our Wholegrain Digital blog (http://bkaprt.com/swd/08-22/).

To wrap up, your greatest resource is your own motivation to take action. In the words of Greta Thunberg, "No one is too small to make a difference."

REFERENCES

Shortened URLs are numbered sequentially; the related long URLs are listed below for reference.

Introduction

00-01 http://bkaprt.com/swd/00-01/

Chapter 1

01-01 https://www.nature.com/articles/d41586-018-06610-y

01-02 https://ec.europa.eu/jrc/en/publication/fossil-co2-emissions-all-world-countries-2018-report

01-03 https://www.cisco.com/c/en/us/solutions/collateral/executive-perspectives/annual-internet-report/white-paper-c11-741490.html

01-04 https://www.sciencedirect.com/science/article/abs/pii/S095965261733233X

01-05 https://positive-internet.com/

01-06 https://httparchive.org/reports/page-weight

01-07 https://planet4.greenpeace.org/

01-08 https://www.bbc.com/future/article/20200131-why-and-how-does-future-planet-count-carbon

01-09 https://www.wearedonation.com

01-10 https://ecosia.zendesk.com/

01-11 https://chris.bolin.co/offline/

01-12 https://www.ecover.com/timeline/

01-13 https://www.ecover.com/clean-manufacturing/

01-14 https://www.campaignlive.co.uk/article/allmodcomms-cleans-1m-ecover-campaign/508936

01-15 https://www.thedrum.com/news/2019/06/12/the-green-market-gets-crowded-ecover-doubling-down-brand-innovation

01-16 https://www.fastcompany.com/90280950/exclusive-patagonia-is-in-business-to-save-our-home-planet

01-17 https://www.patagonia.com/materials/

01-18 https://eu.patagonia.com/gb/en/how-we-fund/international-grant/

01-19 https://www.onepercentfortheplanet.org

01-20 https://www.patagonia.com/films/

01-21 https://wornwear.patagonia.com/

01-22 https://eu.patagonia.com/gb/en/stories/dont-buy-this-jacket-black-friday-and-the-new-york-times/story-18615.html

01-23 https://www.motherjones.com/politics/2006/05/origins-anti-litter-campaign

Chapter 2

02-01 https://en.wikipedia.org/wiki/Four-minute_mile

02-02 https://httparchive.org/reports/state-of-the-web#bytesTotal

02-03 https://www.carbonbrief.org/solar-wind-nuclear-amazingly-low-carbon-footprints

02-04 https://www.volker-quaschning.de/datserv/CO_2-spez/index_e.php

02-05 https://www.electricitymap.org/map

02-06 https://docs.google.com/spreadsheets/d/1gQeUwNFHp7ck4AS7r-d_EwfriM-UFoQ6ApBek9n-hqo/edit?usp=sharing

02-07 https://www.websitecarbon.com/

02-08 https://www.apple.com/euro/environment/pdf/a/generic/products/iphone/iPhone_11_PER_sept2019.pdf

02-09 https://dannyvankooten.com/website-carbon-emissions/

02-10 https://www.carbonfootprint.com/

Chapter 3

03-01 https://hsl.lib.umn.edu/

03-02 https://www.stratd.ai

03-03 https://httparchive.org/reports/page-weight#bytesImg

03-04 https://developers.google.com/speed/webp/docs/webp_study

03-05 https://jakearchibald.com/2020/avif-has-landed/

03-06 https://aneventapart.com/news/post/the-joy-of-optimizing-images-by-una-kravets-aea-video

03-07 https://lowimpact.organicbasics.com/gbp#manifesto

03-08 https://www.zdnet.com/article/google-heres-why-dark-mode-massively-extends-your-oled-phones-battery-life/

03-09 https://www.bristol.ac.uk/news/2019/may/rethinking-digital-service-design-.html

03-10 https://airbnb.io/lottie/#/

03-11 https://www.nu-heat.co.uk/renewables/heat-pumps/heat-pumps-vs-boilers-which-is-best/

03-12 https://manifesto.co.uk/the-impact-of-the-digital-industry-measuring-impact/

03-13 https://rsms.me/inter/

03-14 https://v-fonts.com/

Chapter 4

04-01 https://tonsky.me/blog/disenchantment/

04-02 https://wickedleeks.riverford.co.uk/opinion/news-farm-farming/bitcoin-barns-and-butternut-squash

04-03 https://greenlab.di.uminho.pt/wp-content/uploads/2017/10/sleFinal.pdf

04-04 https://benchmarksgame-team.pages.debian.net/benchmarksgame/

04-05 https://www.wholegraindigital.com/blog/guide-to-using-analytics-for-performance-and-privacy/

04-06 https://www.nytimes.com/interactive/2015/10/01/business/cost-of-mobile-ads.html

04-07 https://www.fontsquirrel.com/tools/webfont-generator

04-08 https://fontdrop.info/

04-09 https://everythingfonts.com/subsetter

04-10 https://codekitapp.com/

Chapter 5

05-01 https://www.mdpi.com/2078-1547/6/1/117#abstract

05-02 https://eta-publications.lbl.gov/sites/default/files/lbnl-1005775_v2.pdf

05-03 https://www.meetup.com/GreenTech-South-West/events/271843079/

05-04 https://blog.cloudflare.com/the-climate-and-cloudflare/

05-05 https://www.iea.org/data-and-statistics

05-06 https://biz.loudoun.gov/key-business-sectors/data-centers/

05-07 https://www.greenpeace.org/usa/reports/click-clean-virginia/

05-08 https://www.thegreenwebfoundation.org/

05-09 https://www.lowtechmagazine.com/2020/01/how-sustainable-is-a-solar-powered-website.html

05-10 https://practical.engineering/blog/2019/6/24/how-does-the-power-grid-work

05-11 https://energysavingtrust.org.uk/home-energy-efficiency/switching-utilities/buying-green-electricity

05-12 https://www.ecotricity.co.uk/about-ecotricity/britain-s-greenest-energy-company

05-13 https://www.wired.com/story/amazon-google-micro-
soft-green-clouds-and-hyperscale-data-centers/

05-14 https://www.blog.google/outreach-initiatives/sustainability/internet-24x7-
carbon-free-energy-should-be-too/

05-15 https://electrek.co/2020/07/24/tesla-megapack-project-switch-datacenter/

05-16 https://www.tesla.com/en_GB/support/autobidder

Chapter 6

06-01 https://doteveryone.org.uk/wp-content/uploads/2019/04/PeoplePow-
erTech_Doteveryone_May2019.pdf

06-02 https://www.wholegraindigital.com/blog/3-qualities-of-a-great-team/

06-03 https://media.nesta.org.uk/documents/Sustainability_1.pdf

06-04 https://www.whitehouse.gov/wp-content/uploads/2019/03/ap_19_
it-fy2020.pdf

Chapter 7

07-01 https://science.sciencemag.org/content/308/5727/1431

07-02 https://coastal.climatecentral.org/

07-03 https://ix.cs.uoregon.edu/~ram/papers/ANRW-2018.pdf

07-04 https://www.theregister.co.uk/2018/09/14/hurricane_florence_
data_centers/

07-05 http://theconversation.com/as-flames-encroach-those-at-risk-may-lose-
phone-signal-when-they-need-it-most-126827

07-06 https://earthobservatory.nasa.gov/images/146110/fires-and-smoke-en-
gulf-southeastern-australia

07-07 https://www.abc.net.au/news/rural/2020-01-13/are-australias-telecommu-
nication-up-to-the-new-kind-of-megafire/11860238

07-08 https://blog.cloudflare.com/cloudflare-during-the-coronavi-
rus-emergency/

07-09 https://newrepublic.com/article/155993/can-internet-survive-cli-
mate-change

07-10 https://www.poynter.org/tech-tools/2017/text-only-news-sites-are-slowly-
making-a-comeback-heres-why/

07-11 https://www.gov.uk/coronavirus

07-12 https://digital.gov/

07-13 https://formidable.com/work/starbucks-progressive-web-app/

07-14 https://wefarm.co

07-1 https://www.wholegraindigital.com/curiously-green/issue-2/

Resources

08-01 https://sustainableux.com/

08-02 https://climateaction.tech/

08-03 https://curiously.green/

08-04 https://greeningdigital.substack.com/

08-05 https://heated.world/

08-06 https://www.sustainablewebmanifesto.com/

08-07 https://www.websitecarbon.com/

08-08 https://ecograder.com/

08-09 https://www.performancebudget.io/

08-10 https://www.wholegraindigital.com/blog/granola-2/

08-11 https://imageoptim.com/mac

08-12 https://shortpixel.com/

08-13 https://tinypng.com/

08-14 https://pngmini.com/

08-15 https://wordpress.org/plugins/webp-express/

08-16 https://www.doteveryone.org.uk/project/consequence-scanning/

08-17 https://www.carbonfootprint.com/calculator.aspx

08-18 https://bimpactassessment.net/

08-19 https://www.ipcc.ch/sr15/

08-20 https://www.nature.com/articles/d41586-018-06610-y%20

08-21 https://www.mdpi.com/2078-1547/6/1/117

08-22 https://www.wholegraindigital.com/blog/

INDEX

ABOUT A BOOK APART

We cover the emerging and essential topics in web design and development with style, clarity, and above all, brevity—because working designer-developers can't afford to waste time.

COLOPHON

The text is set in FF Yoga and its companion, FF Yoga Sans, both by Xavier Dupré. Headlines and cover are set in Titling Gothic by David Berlow.

This book was printed in Germany using FSC certified papers.